Internet and Social Media Addiction

Addictions

ReferencePoint
Press®

San Diego, CA

Other books in the Compact Research Addictions set:

Gambling Addiction
Heroin Addiction
Sex and Pornography Addictions
Synthetic Drug Addiction

*For a complete list of titles please visit www.referencepointpress.com.

Internet and Social Media Addiction

Andrea C. Nakaya

Addictions

ReferencePoint
Press®

San Diego, CA

© 2015 ReferencePoint Press, Inc.
Printed in the United States

For more information, contact:
ReferencePoint Press, Inc.
PO Box 27779
San Diego, CA 92198
www.ReferencePointPress.com

Picture credits:
Cover: Thinkstock Images
© Kim Kyung-Hoon/Reuters/Corbis: 12
© Owen Franken/Corbis: 17
Maury Aaseng: 31–33, 44–45, 57–60, 72–74

LIBRARY OF CONGRESS CATALOGING-IN-PUBLICATION DATA

Nakaya, Andrea C., 1976–
    Internet and social media addiction / by Andrea C. Nakaya.
        pages cm. -- (Compact research series)
    Includes bibliographical references and index.
    Audience: Grade 9 to 12
    ISBN 978-1-60152-760-8 (hardback) -- ISBN 1-60152-760-8 (hardback)
 1. Internet addiction. 2. Social media addiction. I. Title.
    RC569.5.I54N35   2015
    616.85'84--dc23
                                                                    2014026932

Contents

Foreword 6

Internet and Social Media Addiction at a Glance 8

Overview 10

Is Internet and Social Media Addiction a
    Serious Problem? 20
    Primary Source Quotes 27
    Facts and Illustrations 30

What Causes Online Addiction? 34
    Primary Source Quotes 40
    Facts and Illustrations 43

How Do Online Addictions Affect Health and
    Well-Being? 47
    Primary Source Quotes 53
    Facts and Illustrations 56

How Can People Overcome Internet and
    Social Media Addiction? 61
    Primary Source Quotes 68
    Facts and Illustrations 71

Key People and Advocacy Groups 76

Chronology 78

Related Organizations 80

For Further Research 83

Source Notes 86

List of Illustrations 89

Index 90

About the Author 96

Foreword

"**Where is the knowledge we have lost in information?**"

—T.S. Eliot, "The Rock."

As modern civilization continues to evolve, its ability to create, store, distribute, and access information expands exponentially. The explosion of information from all media continues to increase at a phenomenal rate. By 2020 some experts predict the worldwide information base will double every seventy-three days. While access to diverse sources of information and perspectives is paramount to any democratic society, information alone cannot help people gain knowledge and understanding. Information must be organized and presented clearly and succinctly in order to be understood. The challenge in the digital age becomes not the creation of information, but how best to sort, organize, enhance, and present information.

ReferencePoint Press developed the *Compact Research* series with this challenge of the information age in mind. More than any other subject area today, researching current issues can yield vast, diverse, and unqualified information that can be intimidating and overwhelming for even the most advanced and motivated researcher. The *Compact Research* series offers a compact, relevant, intelligent, and conveniently organized collection of information covering a variety of current topics ranging from illegal immigration and deforestation to diseases such as anorexia and meningitis.

The series focuses on three types of information: objective single-author narratives, opinion-based primary source quotations, and facts and statistics. The clearly written objective narratives provide context and reliable background information. Primary source quotes are carefully selected and cited, exposing the reader to differing points of view, and facts and statistics sections aid the reader in evaluating perspectives. Presenting these key types of information creates a richer, more balanced learning experience.

For better understanding and convenience, the series enhances information by organizing it into narrower topics and adding design features that make it easy for a reader to identify desired content. For example, in *Compact Research: Illegal Immigration*, a chapter covering the economic impact of illegal immigration has an objective narrative explaining the various ways the economy is impacted, a balanced section of numerous primary source quotes on the topic, followed by facts and full-color illustrations to encourage evaluation of contrasting perspectives.

The ancient Roman philosopher Lucius Annaeus Seneca wrote, "It is quality rather than quantity that matters." More than just a collection of content, the *Compact Research* series is simply committed to creating, finding, organizing, and presenting the most relevant and appropriate amount of information on a current topic in a user-friendly style that invites, intrigues, and fosters understanding.

Internet and Social Media Addiction at a Glance

Prevalence

Internet use is extremely widespread; researchers believe that between 1 and 8 percent of users become addicted.

Addiction in Asia

In South Korea, China, and Taiwan, Internet addiction is seen as a serious public health problem, and the governments of these nations have instituted various education and treatment programs to combat it.

Symptoms

To addicts the Internet is more important than school, work, friends, or family. Some may experience withdrawal symptoms such as anxiety or depression if they stop using the Internet.

Recognition by the Medical Community

Internet addiction is not recognized as an official medical disorder in the United States because there is not enough supporting research, and some critics believe it may be a symptom of other problems rather than a distinct disorder.

Causes

Possible causes of addiction include genetic differences, the desire to escape reality, mental health problems, and the increasing accessibility of the Internet due to smartphones.

Effects

Internet addiction can cause both physical and emotional problems and have a negative impact on personal relationships and social development.

Profiting from Addiction

Some companies that provide Internet services actually encourage addiction because it makes their sites more profitable. Some of these companies spend thousands of dollars researching how to make their sites even more addictive.

Treatment Options

Very few treatment centers dedicated to Internet addiction exist in the United States; most are expensive and generally not covered by insurance.

Most Effective Treatment

Common treatments for Internet addiction include learning to set limits and manage Internet use, undertaking cognitive behavior therapy, and addressing underlying problems. Some Asian countries employ military-style boot camps as a common method of treatment.

Overview

“Internet addiction . . . interferes with normal living and causes severe stress on family, friends, loved ones, and one's work environment.”

—Center for Internet Addiction, an organization that provides information and treatment for people suffering from Internet addiction.

“The notion of 'Internet addiction' is shaky at best.”

—Kent Anderson, founder of the opinion blog *Scholarly Kitchen*.

In 2014 filmmakers Shosh Shlam and Hilla Medalia released the documentary *Web Junkie*, set inside the Internet Addiction Treatment Center in China's Daxing County. The military style boot camp near Beijing is one of hundreds like it in China, where young people are sent to be treated for Internet addiction. Most of the youth are sent against their will and in many cases end up there after being tricked or even drugged by their parents. Treatment in the camp includes harsh military-style discipline, medication, therapy sessions, and strenuous physical activity. This tough treatment is widely considered necessary in China, where Internet addiction is believed to be a major threat to the population. In *Web Junkie*, one of the program administrators warns that Internet addiction is as strong as a junkie's craving for drugs. "That's why we call it electronic heroin,"[1] he says. China is one of the few countries in the world to classify Internet addiction as a clinical disorder; however, concern about this issue is not limited to China. Recognition of Internet and social media addiction is worldwide, as is concern over its impact on society and how it should be addressed.

Prevalence of Internet and Social Media Use

Internet and social media use is extremely common in the United States and around the world. In 2012, according to the United States Census Bureau, 74.8 percent of US households had a computer, and approximately 95 percent of those use it to connect to the Internet. The Telecommunication Development Sector, a United Nations agency dedicated to improving telecommunication equipment and networks in developing countries, estimates that as of 2014 approximately 78 percent of people in developed nations use the Internet. While developing nations lag behind, they are catching up; in 2014 approximately 32 percent of those in developing nations were Internet users, an increase from about 21 percent in 2010.

> Internet and social media use is extremely common in the United States and around the world.

People use the Internet for a variety of reasons, including communication, shopping, banking, and entertainment. Online activity is becoming increasingly integral to many parts of life. In 2013 and 2014 the Pew Research Center interviewed more than two thousand technology experts and found that most believe the Internet will eventually become embedded in nearly every part of personal and social life. Pew says, "[In the future] accessing the Internet will be effortless and most people will tap into it so easily it will flow through their lives 'like electricity.'"[2]

An Addiction for Some

Many people believe that addiction to the Internet is possible. Definitions of exactly what constitutes Internet addiction differ widely, but experts generally agree that addicts spend large amounts of time online and that using the Internet becomes one of the most important things in their lives. In 1998 psychiatrist Kimberly Young created a self-assessment test that is widely used by Internet addiction researchers. According to the test, indications of addiction include the need to spend more and more time on the Internet, unsuccessful efforts to reduce Internet use; using the Internet to escape problems or unhappiness; lying about the

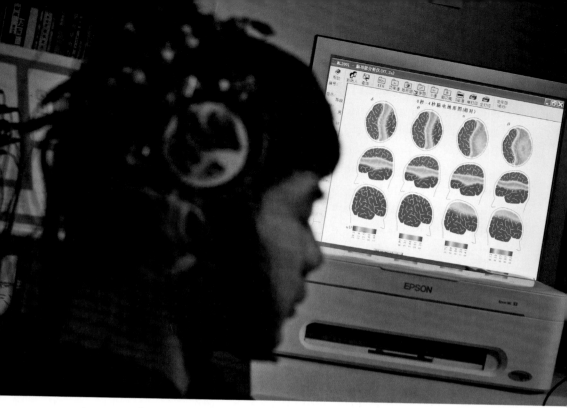

A teenage boy undergoes a brain scan at the Internet Addiction Treatment Center in China. China has hundreds of military-style boot camps similar to this one where young people are sent for treatment of Internet addiction.

extent of one's Internet use; and feeling restless, moody, and irritable when attempting to reduce time online.

Rates of addiction are difficult to determine, and estimates vary widely depending on the country being studied and the way researchers define addiction. Some analysts believe rates are extremely high. For example, the Center for Internet Addiction estimates that 1 in 8 Americans—or 12.5 percent—experience problematic Internet use. Other estimates indicate lower addiction rates—between 1 and 8 percent of the population.

Recognition as an Official Disorder

Although many people experience problems controlling their Internet use, and talk about being addicted is common, widespread disagreement about whether Internet addiction is a true medical disorder still exists. As a result, Internet Addiction Disorder (IAD) has not been classified as an official disorder in the United States. Officially recognized addictions are listed in the *Diagnostic and Statistical Manual of Mental Disorders (DSM)*, a publication of the American Psychological Association (APA). At present almost all of the addictions classified in the *DSM* stem from the abuse of substances such as alcohol and drugs; gambling is the only behavioral addiction the APA recognizes. There is extensive disagreement over whether IAD should be added to the manual. Many experts insist that Internet addiction is a serious medical condition just like problem gambling or alcoholism and needs to be recognized as such. However, others argue that overuse of the Internet is not a true addiction but merely a symptom of other problems or a lack of self-control.

In 2013, with its most recent edition of the *DSM*, the APA took a step toward recognizing IAD by including something called Internet Use Gaming Disorder in the appendix. The APA describes this condition as follows: "The 'gamers' play compulsively, to the exclusion of other interests, and their persistent and recurrent online activity re-

> " **Rates of addiction are difficult to determine, and estimates vary widely.** "

sults in clinically significant impairment or distress."[3] Internet Use Gaming Disorder's place in the appendix does not mean that the APA formally recognizes it as a disorder. Instead, it is included as a condition warranting more detailed study.

Dopamine and Addiction

Dopamine is a neurotransmitter produced by the brain, and it plays an important role in addiction. Researchers have found that certain behaviors—including Internet use—stimulate the release of dopamine, and this release creates a feeling of pleasure. A person can become addicted to whatever caused the dopamine release, engaging in that behavior again and again in order to re-experience the pleasurable feeling. Numerous addictions are related to dopamine release, including alcoholism and drug addiction. For some people the desire for the high they feel from dopamine is so strong that they develop a craving for it and become anxious and unhappy when they cannot get it. This is why the object of addiction becomes more important to addicts than anything else in their lives.

Research shows that numerous aspects of Internet use can stimulate the brain to release dopamine, including its visual stimulation, the promise of rewards, and its unpredictability. Internet rewards take various forms, including reaching a new gaming level, accessing interesting content, or receiving a pleasurable e-mail or posting on one's social media page. Part of what makes these rewards so addicting and keeps users engaged is that they are unpredictable; users are never sure when they will receive their rewards. As Hilarie Cash, cofounder of reSTART, an Internet addiction recovery center, explains, it is common to feel, "I never know what the next tweet is going to be. Who's sent me an e-mail? What will I find with the next click of the mouse? What's waiting for me?"[4] As a result, people spend large amounts of time on the Internet waiting for those rewards.

Is Internet and Social Media Addiction a Serious Problem?

There is widespread disagreement over whether Internet and social media addiction is a serious problem. Some people insist that the threat of Internet addiction has been greatly exaggerated. They argue that it is normal to spend large amounts of time online because the Internet is becoming increasingly central to communication, shopping, entertainment, and myriad other facets of life. Allen Frances, psychiatrist and professor emeritus at Duke University, insists that all this time online does not equal addiction. He says, "It should not be counted as a mental disorder and be called an 'addiction' just because you really love an activity, get a lot of pleasure from it, and spend a lot of time doing it." Frances argues that for most people, using the Internet has an overall positive impact, providing enjoyment and increasing productivity. He says, "This is more love affair and/or tool using than enslavement and is not best considered the stuff of mental disorder."[5]

> " There is widespread disagreement over whether Internet and social media addiction is a serious problem. "

However, some critics warn that many people who spend large amounts of time online actually do so because they are addicted. They argue that this is becoming an increasingly common problem. Greg Beato, contributing editor for *Reason* magazine, worries that because the Internet is such an integral part of most people's lives, everyone is at risk for this addiction. Referring to one of the few groups of people in the United States who generally avoid technology, he warns, "As the Internet weaves itself more and more tightly into our lives, only the Amish are safe."[6]

Video Game Addiction

Video gaming is a common online activity, and one commonly associated with addiction. In fact, many treatment centers that focus on Internet addiction report that a large percentage of the people they treat are gamers. For instance, the reSTART Internet addiction treatment center near Seattle says that most of its patients suffer from a compulsion to play video games, including online games. In China many of the youth that are sent to the country's hundreds of addiction boot camps are gamers.

Researchers have found that one of the most popular and addicting types of online games is Massively Multiplayer Online Role-Playing Games (MMORPGs). In these games people from all over the world interact and compete in a virtual world, forming groups, competing in tournaments, and completing quests. *World of Warcraft* is one of the most popular MMORPGs. Other popular games include *Everquest* and *Guild Wars*. These games are extremely addicting because they contain so many things to do and goals to achieve. In an online forum one gamer explains, "There's always a new item to be had or quest to be done. There are so many activities in these games that can consume your whole day in a heartbeat."[7] In addition, the game world continues to develop even when players are logged off, making them want to keep checking in to see what they are missing.

Online Gambling Addiction

Online gambling is widespread in the United States despite the fact that it is illegal in most states. New Jersey, Delaware, and Nevada are the only states that have legalized online gambling. It is, however, legal in many other parts of the world, so thousands of easily accessible gambling websites exist. The American Gaming Association (AGA) says, "[Despite laws banning gambling] millions of Americans have continued to bet billions of dollars a year at offshore websites. Americans like to gamble online and have demonstrated that they will do so even if their government tells them it is illegal."[8] The organization reports that in 2012 Americans spent $2.6 billion on illegal offshore gambling websites.

Gambling has long existed in society; however, the rise of the Internet has dramatically changed this activity. Journalist Bill Davidow explains, "In the past, society has been able to put physical barriers in place to make it more difficult to satisfy unhealthy obsessions [such as gambling]. For example, gambling casinos were primarily segregated in Nevada. Things are very different today. In the first place, there is no physical barrier between people and the obsession in question. Smartphones and portable electronic devices travel with us in our pockets."[9] Davidow and others worry that the ease of online gambling will lead to a dramatic increase in gambling addiction.

The Widespread Appeal of Social Media

One of the most common online activities is social networking. People use social networking sites to connect with each other for many different reasons. Sites such as Facebook facilitate connection with friends. Other people use sites like LinkedIn for networking in their career field or finding a new job. Some networking sites allow people to connect with groups sharing similar interests; for example, Instagram allows users to share images and videos. Research shows that large numbers of people engage in some type of social networking. In a 2013 survey the Pew Research Center found that 73 percent of online Americans now use a social networking site of some kind, and 42 percent use multiple sites. In 2011 research company comScore surveyed people in 171 countries and found that 1.2 billion people around the world use social networking sites. The company says, "Despite significant differences in government, infrastructure, availability of internet access and cultural practices around the world, social networking is growing in every single country. . . . Regardless of how open or closed a society may be, it is safe to assume that more than half of local online populations are engaging in online social networking."[10]

> " Research shows that large numbers of people engage in some type of social networking. "

The popularity of various social networking sites is ever changing,

Interaction via social media has widespread appeal among teens and adults worldwide. It offers any number of benefits but can, in some instances, become an obsession.

and new sites are created every year. However, Facebook dominates all other social networking sites. Launched in 2004, Facebook now has more than a billion members worldwide and is the leading social networking site in most countries. Other popular social networking sites include Blogger, Twitter, Instagram, and Snapchat.

What Causes Online Addiction?

Researchers who do believe that addiction to the Internet or social media is possible disagree over what might be its causes. Some believe addiction is the result of genetics, such as variations in brain chemistry or development or gender differences. Others argue that addiction is due to the nature of the Internet itself—a highly engaging and stimulating medium that is difficult to stay away from. Still others place the blame on the spread of smartphones, which make the Internet easily accessible from almost anywhere. Some critics insist that Internet addiction is not actually a true medical condition but merely a symptom of various types of personal problems and mental health disorders such as anxiety or depression.

How Do Online Addictions Affect Health and Well-Being?

Some people believe that spending large amounts of time online can cause harm to people's health and well-being. For example, the Bradford Regional Medical Center, which founded one of the first inpatient treatment programs for Internet addiction in the United States, describes a downward spiral of harm. It says, "Internet addicts struggle to control their behaviors, and experience despair over their constant failure to do so. Their loss of self-esteem grows, fueling the need to escape even further into their addictive behaviors. A sense of powerlessness pervades the lives of addicts."[11]

> " **Some researchers believe addiction is the result of genetics.** "

Others contend that living life constantly connected to the Internet is a new trend that will become increasingly common in the future and is not necessarily harmful. Journalist Tony Dokoupil points out that because the Internet is such an important part of life and work, the majority of people actually qualify as addicts. He says, "Don't kid yourself: the gap between an 'Internet addict' and John Q. Public is thin to nonexistent." For example, he says, "One of the early flags for addiction was spending more than 38 hours a week online. By that definition, we are all addicts now, many of us by Wednesday afternoon, Tuesday if it's a busy week."[12] Critics argue that while some people may experience harm from that constant connection, for many others it actually makes life more productive and more enjoyable.

Profiting from Addiction

Some businesses work hard to profit from people's interest in being online. The individuals and companies that create social networking sites, games, and various other online activities make large amounts of money by attracting people to their websites and keeping them there as long as possible. Addiction is good for their business. As a result these companies are investing time and millions of dollars to understand how to make their sites more attractive. For example, journalist Steve Henn talks about game makers. He says, "As we play games, game developers are tracking every click, running tests and analyzing data. They are trying to find out: What can they tweak to make us play just a bit longer?"[13]

As research techniques become increasingly sophisticated, critics worry that the problem of Internet addiction will grow. Davidow warns, "As companies learn how to use neuroscience to make virtual environments more appealing, that number [of people who are addicted to the Internet] will undoubtedly increase." While some people argue that such exploitation is morally wrong, Davidow points out that it is inevitable because of the huge potential for profit that comes with addiction. He says, "The leaders of Internet companies face an interesting . . . imperative: either they hijack neuroscience to gain market share and make large profits, or they let competitors do that and run away with the market."[14]

> " Some businesses work hard to profit from people's interest in being online. "

How Can People Overcome Internet and Social Media Addiction?

As fears about Internet addiction become increasingly common, so do suggestions about how people can overcome addiction. In most countries—including the United States—only a few treatment centers focus specifically on Internet addiction. However, as awareness of the problem grows the number of treatment facilities is gradually increasing. Some Asian countries view Internet addiction as more of a threat and have taken a far more aggressive approach to the problem. For example, South Korea has government-sponsored counseling for addicts and widespread education programs to prevent addiction developing in youth. The Chinese government also funds treatment for addiction.

The Internet is a relatively new technology, and the concept of Internet addiction is even newer. As a result society is still debating questions such as whether it exists, what causes it, how it affects people, and whether it is something that society should—or even can—try to change. The answers to these questions are important because every year the Internet becomes increasingly central to the lives of people all over the world.

Is Internet and Social Media Addiction a Serious Problem?

> **Internet addiction is a serious problem.**
>
> —Larry D. Rosen, research psychologist and expert in technology issues.

> **I have some doubts about the notion that there can be an Internet addiction.**
>
> —Keith Hampton, sociologist and assistant professor at the Annenberg School for Communication at the University of Pennsylvania.

In 1995 psychiatrist Ivan Goldberg posted a new disorder called Internet Addiction Disorder on the psychiatry bulletin board at the popular website psych.com. Symptoms included giving up important social activities because of Internet use and unsuccessful efforts to control Internet use. A large number of people responded to his posting, recognizing themselves as addicts and asking for help. The problem was that Goldberg did not actually believe in such a disorder; he had created the posting as a joke. However, Goldberg's joke had lasting effects. It provoked recognition and discussion about overuse of the Internet and social media. People around the world continue to debate whether such an addiction is possible and whether it is a serious problem.

Experts disagree over whether IAD is a true medical disorder. Many insist that it is. For example, in a 2012 edition of *Current Psychiatry Reviews* a group of experts review the existing research and report that IAD is a serious worldwide problem with recognizable symptoms. They state, "It is accompanied by changes in mood, preoccupation with the Internet and digital media, the inability to control the amount of time spent interfacing with digital technology, the need for more time or a new game to achieve a desired mood, [and] withdrawal symptoms when not engaged."[15] The researchers argue that the medical community should develop uniform diagnostic criteria for this addiction.

However, critics counter that while many people do indeed use the Internet excessively, overuse does not qualify as a serious medical disorder. Allen Frances insists that while obsessive use can be problematic, spending large amounts of time doing something does not mean a person is clinically addicted. Frances is opposed to recognizing IAD as an official medical condition in the *DSM* because he believes it will lead to overdiagnoses of addictions. "Where do you draw the line?" he asks, "Why not include work addiction, sex addiction, shopping addiction, golf addiction, model-railroading addiction?"[16]

Comparison with Substance Addictions

Many people believe that Internet and social media addiction resembles addiction to substances such as alcohol and drugs. The Bradford Regional Medical Center explains the similarities. It says, "Individuals addicted to alcohol or other drugs . . . develop a relationship with their chemical(s) of choice—a relationship that takes precedence over any and all other aspects of their lives. Addicts find they need drugs merely to feel normal. In internet addiction, a parallel situation exists. The internet, like food or drugs in other addictions, provides the high and addicts become dependent on this cyberspace high."[17]

Physician and gamer Andrew P. Doan says that like drug and alcohol addicts, Internet addicts will do almost anything—regardless of the harm it causes themselves and others—to continue their addiction. He gives the example of gamers. Doan says, "Like a cocaine junkie, video game addicts will

> "Critics argue that while many people do indeed use the Internet excessively, overuse does not qualify as a serious medical disorder.

do things to keep playing that they would never do in their right minds. . . . It is common for addicts to pretend to be sick so they can skip work, lie to loved ones to get out of commitments, and many other uncharacteristic behaviors, all so they can keep their digital drug flowing."[18] An extreme example of such behavior occurred in 2007 when seventeen-year-old Daniel Petric shot both his parents after they took away his *Halo 3* game.

Addiction Statistics

Among researchers who believe that Internet addiction is a true medical disorder, prevalence statistics vary widely, as do the criteria. In a 2010 article in the *American Journal of Drug and Alcohol Abuse* researchers reviewed literature published between 2000 and 2009 and found that the United States and Europe have Internet addiction rates of between 1.5 percent and 8.2 percent of the population. In some Asian countries with high rates of Internet access, the numbers are estimated to be much higher. For instance, in 2010 *China Daily* reported that as many as 15 percent of eighteen- to twenty-three-year-olds were addicted.

> **Many people believe that Internet and social media addiction resembles addiction to substances such as alcohol and drugs.**

Critics contend that numbers such as these greatly exaggerate the extent of the problem. They believe Internet addiction is overestimated because researchers do not measure it correctly. Mark Griffiths from Nottingham Trent University in the United Kingdom explains, "I've been really highly critical of prevalence surveys. . . . [They] measure preoccupation rather than addiction."[19] He argues that true addiction involves not just preoccupation with something but also other symptoms, including negative effects on a person's life and withdrawal symptoms if they stop. He says that when these criteria are used, the number of people who are truly addicted to the Internet is actually very small.

Addiction Experiences

Numerous stories from Internet users reveal that regardless of whether it is possible to become truly addicted, for some people Internet use can become a very serious problem, destroying lives and even leading to thoughts of suicide. For example, Stacey, a Washington mother of two, says she became addicted to an online game called "Spades." According to Stacey, she was consumed by the game. She says, "All I could think about was going back and playing on the computer again. So, even if I was physically present [elsewhere], my brain was still on the computer."[20] Eventually her husband divorced her and took the children with him. Another gamer, Ryan Van Cleave, a writer and college professor, not only lost his job and some of his friends because of his addiction, but he even thought about killing himself. Van Cleave says he was playing the online game *World of Warcraft* for up to eighty hours a week, and that his life was falling apart. "My kids hate me. My wife is threatening (again) to leave me." Van Cleave adds, "And I am perpetually exhausted from skipping sleep so I can play more Warcraft."[21] One day, after an eighteen-hour gaming session, he found himself standing on a bridge contemplating suicide because he was so unhappy.

> "Among researchers who believe that Internet addiction is a true medical disorder, prevalence statistics vary widely, as do the criteria."

Too Much Online Gaming

Some people believe that online gaming is one of the most dangerous types of Internet use because people often play for hours a day, becoming so engrossed in their game worlds that they ignore everything else. Some gamers become so immersed in gaming that they report playing for hours without eating, drinking, or sleeping; even wearing diapers so they do not have to stop playing to go to the bathroom. In 2012 two Taiwanese gamers died after marathon game-playing sessions. Eighteen-year-old Chuang reportedly died after playing *Diablo III* for forty consecutive hours at an Internet café. Chen Rong-yu also died at an Internet café after a long gaming session.

While the deaths of the Taiwanese gamers illustrate the notion that gaming can be harmful, critics argue that spending hours playing online games is not necessarily a serious problem. Elias Aboujaoude, who runs

Stanford University's Obsessive Compulsive Disorder Clinic and Impulse Control Disorders Clinic contends that spending hours on the Internet does not equal a serious addiction. Instead, he says, a person needs to examine how that time is affecting the rest of his or her life. He says, "You look at the offline effects, not so much at what the person is doing online or how much time they're spending in front of their browser."[22] Aboujaoude and some other critics believe that if hours of gaming do not have a harmful impact on the rest of a person's life, then that gaming is not a cause for serious concern.

Gambling

Some people believe that online gambling poses a serious threat to society because it is so easy to access. Individuals no longer need to travel to a casino to gamble; instead, they can gamble from anyplace with Internet access—or, with a smartphone, from almost anywhere at all, any time of the day or night. Charles "C.P." Mirarchi is a former compulsive gambler turned counselor at the Collingswood Nursing & Rehabilitation Center in Maryland. "The access scares me," he says, "I had a guy come in after a phone call because he was playing poker for four days straight on his phone."[23]

Others contend that online gambling is a serious problem only because it is largely illegal in the United States. They insist that legalizing and regulating online gambling could greatly reduce the problem of addiction. The American Gaming Association (AGA) says that other countries have managed to do this: "Numerous Western nations—including the United Kingdom, France, Italy, and some provinces in Canada—have created structures for tight regulation of the online gambling industry."[24] According to the AGA, strict regulation helps exclude underage gamers and gives problem gamers resources that help them limit their play or keep away from gambling websites.

> " **Individuals no longer need to travel to a casino to gamble; instead, they can gamble from anyplace with Internet access.** "

Social Media

Numerous studies show that large numbers of people are extremely attached to social networking and spend hours every day participating in this online activity. Critics worry that social media addiction is a serious problem. Alexandra Reed, a thirty-nine-year-old mother from Charlotte, North Carolina, says she checks her social networking accounts all the time through her cell phone. She says, "Even when I'm driving, I might have Facebook open." As Reed told an interviewer, "At a red light the first thing I (do is) just look at my phone. I get a little anxious if I see a notification and don't read it."[25] Research shows that Reed's constant need to check her social networking sites is not uncommon.

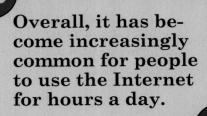

Overall, it has become increasingly common for people to use the Internet for hours a day.

Critics insist that this is not a serious problem because it actually makes life better by encouraging and enhancing communication. Technology expert Zeynep Tufekci argues that "Texting, Facebook-status updates, and Twitter conversations are not displacing face-to-face socializing—on average, they are making them stronger."[26]

Addiction in Asia

While the seriousness of Internet addiction is still widely debated in the United States, a number of Asian countries agree that it is a serious problem. In China, Taiwan, and South Korea, a large majority of people own smartphones and other devices that give them easy access to the Internet. With that access have come high levels of attachment. For example, journalist Youkyung Lee relates the case of Park Jung-in, a South Korean girl who is with her smartphone day and night. Lee says, "Park Jung-in, an 11-year-old South Korean, sleeps with her Android smartphone instead of a teddy bear. . . . Throughout the day, the gadget is in her hands whether she is in school, in the restroom or in the street as she constantly types messages to her friends. . . . 'I get nervous when the battery falls below 20 percent,' Park said as she fiddled with the palm-size gadget. 'I find it stressful to stay out of the wireless hotspot zone for too long.'"[27]

In a survey released in 2012 the South Korean government estimated that approximately 2.55 million people there were addicted to their smartphones. Recognizing the harms of addiction, the South Korean government has instituted various efforts to combat the problem, including education, counseling, and rehabilitation centers. South Korea is not the only Asian country to officially recognize Internet addiction as a serious problem. China, Japan, and Taiwan have taken similar action.

Overall, it has become increasingly common for people to use the Internet for hours a day. The debate, however, is whether extensive use of the Internet equals addiction and whether it is a serious problem.

Primary Source Quotes*

Is Internet and Social Media Addiction a Serious Problem?

66 **Many studies have confirmed the existence of compulsive or addictive use of the internet.** 99

—David Greenfield, "The Addictive Properties of Internet Usage," in Kimberly S. Young and Cristiano Nabuco de Abreu, eds., *Internet Addiction: A Handbook and Guide to Evaluation and Treatment.* Hoboken, NJ: Wiley, 2010, p. 135.

Greenfield is an Internet addiction expert and founder of the Center for Internet and Technology Addiction.

66 **It's not a clear enough syndrome that you can say at this point . . . [Internet addiction is] clearly a disease— that it's an illness or a sickness. . . . We have to have more evidence.** 99

—Charles O'Brien, interview by John D. Sutter, "Is 'Gaming Addiction' a Real Disorder?," *CNN*, August 6, 2012. www.cnn.com.

O'Brien is a professor of psychiatry at the University of Pennsylvania. He was part of the task force that worked on the 2013 update of the American Psychological Association's *Diagnostic and Statistical Manual of Mental Disorders.*

Bracketed quotes indicate conflicting positions.

* Editor's Note: While the definition of a primary source can be narrowly or broadly defined, for the purposes of Compact Research, a primary source consists of: 1) results of original research presented by an organization or researcher; 2) eyewitness accounts of events, personal experience, or work experience; 3) first-person editorials offering pundits' opinions; 4) government officials presenting political plans and/or policies; 5) representatives of organizations presenting testimony or policy.

❝Despite all the media hype, it is way premature to conclude that the Internet is controlling our lives, ruining our brains, and driving us crazy. We are not all Internet addicts.❞

—Allen Frances, "Internet Addiction: The Next New Fad Diagnosis," *Huffington Post*, August 13, 2012. www.huffingtonpost.com.

Frances is a psychiatrist and professor emeritus at Duke University. He was chairman of the task force that created the 2013 update of the American Psychological Association's *Diagnostic and Statistical Manual of Mental Disorders.*

❝The number of people with a problem related to gaming and use of other devices is growing exponentially in the U.S. and around the world. . . . Clearly, the problem is getting out of control.❞

—Kevin Roberts, "Confessions of a Cyber Junkie," *USA Today*, March 2011. www.usatoday.com.

Roberts is a recovering Internet addict and author of *Cyber Junkie: Escape the Gaming and Internet Trap.*

❝People have become addicted to the use of social media. These addictions are becoming very serious and have become equated with addictions to hard drugs like heroin and crack cocaine.❞

—Colin Woods, "Social Media Junkies," *Problems with Social Media (Longwood Blogs)*, May 29, 2014. http://blogs.longwood.edu.

Woods writes a blog about social media.

❝Some of you . . . may not believe that video games are addictive and may not agree that video game addiction is a real illness. . . . Let my story be a lesson to you. Video game addiction almost destroyed my marriage, my family, and my medical career. It almost took my life.❞

—Andrew P. Doan, with Brooke Strickland, *Hooked on Games: The Lure and Cost of Video Game and Internet Addiction.* Coralville, IA: F.E.P. International, 2012, p. 183.

Doan has a degree in neuroscience and is an expert in technology and video game addiction.

66 I do not have any doubts that some people do have problems with a healthy internet use, but the concept of addiction seems not to be the right one here.**99**

—Mario Lehenbauer-Baum, "Nomophobia—the Hype About an Artificially Created Disorder," *Thrive in Life* (blog), March 9, 2014. www.drlehenbauer.com.

Lehenbauer-Baum is a clinical psychologist and motivational speaker.

66 Gambling has benefits but also has well documented negative consequences. Internet gambling is no exception. It is clear that some who gamble online will develop problems and that these problems are serious.**99**

—National Council on Problem Gambling, "Internet Responsible Gambling Standards," April 23, 2012. www.npcgambling.org.

The National Council on Problem Gambling was created in 1972. It advocates for programs and services to assist problem gamblers and their families.

66 The tools have been developed to regulate online gambling effectively . . . ensuring that bets are not accepted from jurisdictions where online gambling is prohibited, barring money laundering, and providing tools for the customers themselves to control their own gambling.**99**

—David O. Stewart, "Online Gaming Five Years After UIGEA," *American Gaming Association*, 2011. www.americangaming.org.

Stewart is a lawyer and an expert in gaming law.

Is Internet and Social Media Addiction a Serious Problem?

- The Telecommunication Development Sector, a United Nations agency dedicated to improving telecommunication equipment and networks in developing countries, estimates that in 2014, **2.9 billion people** around the world were Internet users.

- According to a 2013 survey by the Pew Research Center of 2,252 US adults, **15 percent** of respondents do not use the Internet or e-mail.

- In a 2013 survey of 1,801 US adults, the Pew Research Center found that **63 percent of Facebook users** visit the site at least once a day, with **40 percent** doing so multiple times throughout the day.

- A Fairleigh Dickinson University PublicMind poll in 2014 found that **27 percent of respondents** support legalizing Internet gambling, while **63 percent** oppose it.

- According to a study published 2012 in *Psychological Science*, in a survey of **250 people** researchers found that urges to keep on top of social networks and work were harder to resist than urges for alcohol or tobacco.

- In a 2012 review of Internet addiction research, Hilarie Cash and other researchers found that estimates of the rate of addiction vary greatly around the world—from **0.3 percent** to **38 percent** of the population.

Online Technology Affects Relationships

The Internet and social media are so pervasive in people's lives that they have a significant impact on interpersonal relationships. These graphs are based on a survey of 2,252 US adults. They show that people who are in committed relationships report that the Internet and cell phones have both positive and negative effects on their lives. For people who have difficulty controlling their Internet and social media use, negative effects are likely to be even greater.

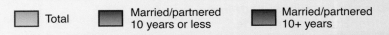

Legend: Total | Married/partnered 10 years or less | Married/partnered 10+ years

Negative Technology Experiences in Relationships

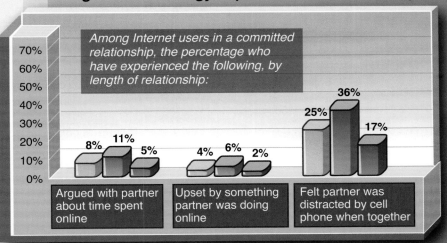

Among Internet users in a committed relationship, the percentage who have experienced the following, by length of relationship:

- Argued with partner about time spent online: 8%, 11%, 5%
- Upset by something partner was doing online: 4%, 6%, 2%
- Felt partner was distracted by cell phone when together: 25%, 36%, 17%

Positive Technology Experiences in Relationships

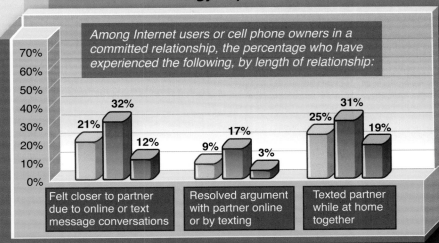

Among Internet users or cell phone owners in a committed relationship, the percentage who have experienced the following, by length of relationship:

- Felt closer to partner due to online or text message conversations: 21%, 32%, 12%
- Resolved argument with partner online or by texting: 9%, 17%, 3%
- Texted partner while at home together: 25%, 31%, 19%

Source: Pew Research Internet Project, "Couples, the Internet, and Social Media," February 11, 2014. www.pewinternet.org.

Signs of Addiction Are Common

According to a recent poll, a significant percentage of people stay online longer than they intend, lose sleep and job productivity because they are online, and sometimes choose the Internet over face-to-face interaction with others. Internet addiction specialists consider all these activities to be possible signs of addiction.

Do you normally stay online longer than you intended?

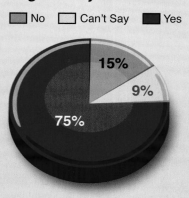

Do you sometimes choose to spend more time online over going out with others?

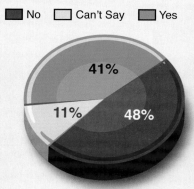

Do you usually lose sleep due to late-night log-ins?

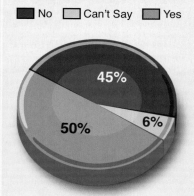

Do you think your job performance or productivity suffers because of the Internet?

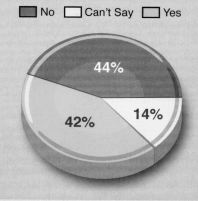

Source: Maps of the World, "Is Internet Addiction Real?—Facts and Infographic," 2013. www.mapsofworld.com.

Internet Takes Highest Priority in People's Lives

If given the choice of going without fast food or giving up the Internet for a year, most people would dump fast food rather than live without their Internet connections. This is the finding of a survey that appeared in the online news site *Huffington Post*. While this in itself is not a sign of addiction, experts say that addicts often demonstrate similar behavior. Their addiction becomes central to their lives—and to feed this addiction they often give up all other daily tasks, needs, and responsibilities.

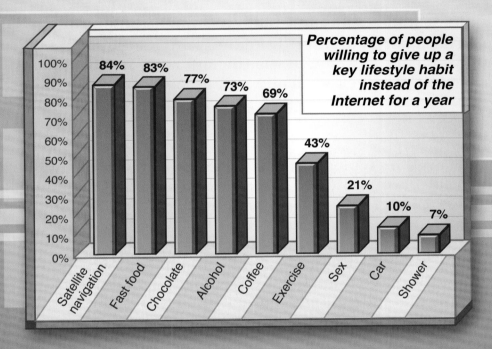

Percentage of people willing to give up a key lifestyle habit instead of the Internet for a year

Source: Courtney Palis, "Internet Economy: How Essential is the Internet to the U.S.?," *Huffington Post*, March 20, 2012. www.huffingtonpost.com.

- According to a 2012 report by the Nielsen research company, in July 2012 consumers spent an average of **520 minutes** a month on the Internet, a **21 percent increase** from the previous year.

- According to the survey of smartphone addiction completed by South Korea's National Information Society Agency in 2012, the percentage of smartphone addiction there was **8.4 percent**.

What Causes
Online Addiction?

66The majority of Internet addicts suffer from emotional problems . . . and will use the fantasy world of the Internet to psychologically escape unpleasant feelings or stressful situations.99

—Center for Internet Addiction Recovery, an organization that provides information and treatment for people suffering from Internet addiction.

66There's no typical Internet addict—just as with drugs or alcohol, addiction can affect anyone, regardless of age, gender or socioeconomic status.99

—Carolyn Gregoire, editor at the *Huffington Post*.

In the United States and most developed nations the majority of people use the Internet extensively. It is not uncommon for people to spend hours every day online and for a wide variety of reasons. However, not everyone exhibits the same control over Internet use. The website Recovery.org explains, "For most people, it's an extremely useful and manageable medium that makes it easy to do everything from conducting extensive research for work or school to watching a full season of a favorite television program in one sitting. However, for some people, the Internet has become the place where they spend most if not all of their time. Their Internet use has spiraled out of control."[28] Some experts define such compulsive use as an addiction, or IAD. However, researchers are not sure why certain people have trouble controlling their Internet use. They continue to examine various possible causes to understand this behavior and to help people better regulate their online and offline lives.

Genetic Differences

Researchers have found that some people may be genetically predisposed to IAD. One possible reason may be that their dopamine systems are different. Dopamine is a neurotransmitter produced by the brain, and certain behaviors, including Internet use, stimulate the brain to release dopamine, resulting in a feeling of pleasure. However some people's brains produce less dopamine than others. Addiction researchers explain, "Individuals with this predisposition . . . [have] difficulty experiencing normal levels of pleasure in activities that most people would find rewarding. To increase pleasure these individuals are more likely to seek greater than average engagement in behaviors that stimulate an increase in dopamine."[29] This means that people whose dopamine systems function this way may be likely to spend more time online than others. Researchers have also found other possible indications of a genetic basis for IAD. For example, in one study they found that a particular gene mutation is more common in problematic Internet users. Another study showed that Internet addicts have less matter in the areas of the brain responsible for memory and decision making.

> " Researchers are not sure why certain people have trouble controlling their Internet use. "

However, critics argue that these types of studies are too small to prove anything and that more research on Internet addiction is needed to properly understand it. Charles O'Brien, a professor of psychiatry at the University of Pennsylvania, argues that too much of the knowledge that exists about this addiction is based on anecdotal evidence, not scientific research. As a result, he says, "There are a lot of things we don't know."[30]

A Way to Escape Reality

There is evidence that some people develop IAD because they are unhappy in their offline lives and turn to the Internet as a way to temporarily escape that unhappiness. Author and recovering Internet addict Kevin Roberts explains, "When I entered the cyber world, I escaped responsibility for a while, as video gaming shut down my mind to everything else. . . . I did not have to think or feel anything real. So much stimulation came at me that there was no opportunity for unpleasantness to worm its way through."[31] The Center for Internet Addiction reports that almost 75 percent of Internet addicts have problems in their relationships with other people and turn to online interaction as an escape.

> **Some people may be genetically predisposed to IAD.**

Some researchers believe this is one of the reasons that IAD is so high among youth in China. China has a very strict and competitive education system, and many youth report that this is a cause of stress. Filmmaker Shosh Shlam was in China to create a documentary about IAD among Chinese youth. She argues that the strict education system, in combination with China's one-child per family policy, creates intense pressure on youth. She says, "Because there is one child and the future of his family is on his shoulders, the parents are pushing and pushing them to be a better student."[32] She believes some youth spend large amounts of time on the Internet as a means of escaping that pressure.

Addiction in College

For some youth, going away to college and being free from parental supervision can cause them to spend large amounts of time using the Internet. College students have large blocks of free time and the ability to spend as much time as they want online without a parent reminding them to take a break or attend to other obligations. In addition, for some youth the stresses of college can contribute to addiction. The website Internet Addiction Resource explains, "Being young and still developing—physically, emotionally, and mentally, young adults in college could end up feeling overwhelmed. And while college can be a fun and adventurous time, it can also be stressful, scary, and lonesome. Making friends could be difficult, and the work load and responsibility could be more than they've handled previously, so they're caught unprepared."[33] Internet Addiction Resource argues some students spend large amounts of time online to escape these stresses.

Gender

A large number of researchers and medical professionals believe males are more likely than females to become addicted to the Internet. For example, Hilarie Cash, cofounder of the reSTART Internet addiction recovery program, believes that addiction is both more common and more serious in men than women. She says that women who do experience addiction problems also tend to function better than men in the rest of their lives, "whereas when the guys get lost in that world, they tend to just jump off the cliff and really go down."[34] In fact, because so few women sought treatment at the reSTART center, it became a male-only program.

However, not all research shows that Internet addiction is more prevalent in males. Researchers from the University of Bonn in Germany recently found evidence that women may actually be genetically more likely to become addicted. They investigated the genetic makeup of people with problematic Internet behavior; that is, those who reported that their thoughts revolved around it and their well-being was harmed if they had to go without it. The researchers compared these users with people who did not experience problematic behavior. They found that problematic Internet users were more likely to carry a certain genetic variation that may contribute to the addiction and that women were more likely to have the mutation.

> " A large number of researchers and medical professionals believe males are more likely than females to become addicted to the Internet. "

Stimulation and Engagement

Experts also disagree over whether the Internet is more addicting than other types of media. Some argue that the Internet is a uniquely stimulating and engaging medium, which makes it pleasurable to use and extremely easy to become addicted to. Stanford University's Elias Aboujaoude says, "When we talk about problematic Internet use, one common complaint is that there's nothing really different about it, that it's similar to, you know, when radio first came around or TV or even novels." But he insists that the Internet is unique. He says, "I really do believe the Internet is different. It's different in that it engages you a lot more. You're immersed in it. It talks back to you."[35] Aboujaoude says that he has seen numerous patients with no history of addictive behavior easily become addicted to the Internet. Tony Schwartz, CEO of The Energy Project and author of *The Way We Work Isn't Working*, agrees, calling the Internet "as addictive as crack." He warns, "If you expose yourself to [the Internet and similar technologies] . . . continuously, they will pull you in the way a drug would—continuously, even when you know it's not serving you well."[36]

Yet critics argue that such fears are not justified. They point out that throughout history new technologies have always been met with suspicion and that such suspicions frequently turn out to be baseless. For instance, when the printed book was invented critics insisted that society was at risk of information overload. In fact, books have proved to be greatly beneficial. It is argued that fears of the Internet will likewise turn out to be exaggerated.

Other Disorders

According to the Center for Internet Addiction, the majority of Internet addicts also suffer from other addictions, such as alcohol, drugs, or sex, or have emotional problems such as mood disorders, depression, or anxiety disorders. The reSTART Internet addiction recovery program reports that each of its patients has a mental health condition in addition to Internet addiction. However, researchers do not completely understand why these addictions often coexist. Some people believe that excessive Internet use is simply a symptom of these other disorders.

The Desire to Be Social

People have an innate desire to be social, and some analysts believe users can become addicted to the Internet because it facilitates social interaction. This seems to be particularly true for those who have difficulty with face-to-face interaction. Cash says that this social factor is an important element of addiction. She says that many of the patients at reSTART say they find it easier to make friends through online games than in person. Cash states, "We're social animals, right? So they find that in these games they can connect with people and try to meet their social needs that way. And that's a huge element in the addiction."[37]

Some people contend, though, that online socialization is not necessarily harmful because in many cases it helps initiate real-world socialization. For example, the organization ParentFurther argues that online interaction can be greatly beneficial to youth by helping them overcome communication fears. It explains, "Kids can gain social confidence from interacting with other people online, which may help them feel more secure in new situations, such as going to college, joining a sports team, and meeting new friends."[38] What some see as addiction, then, may just be a means for Internet users to stay connected to others.

Fueled by Smartphones

It is widely argued that Internet addiction is fueled by the rise of smartphones. The smartphone makes it possible for a person to access the Internet anytime and anywhere, paving the way for addictive behavior. Journalist Sandy Fitzgerald says, "Mobile devices are always nearby, making them more tempting than a PC, which you can walk away from. They also create a habit that's hard to control."[39] Research shows that more than half of Americans have smartphones and that many smartphone owners take advantage of their phone's ability to easily connect them to the Internet. For instance, in a 2012 survey by *Time* magazine and Qualcomm, researchers found that 29 percent of respondents said their device is always the first thing they look at every day. One in five of those surveyed checks his or her smartphone every ten minutes. According to a 2012 study commissioned by the security app Lookout and conducted by Harris Interactive, 30 percent of people check their smartphones during a meal, 24 percent while driving, and 9 percent during religious services or at a house of worship. As the Internet continues to play an increasingly important role in everyday life, researchers work to understand what causes Internet addiction and how to help those people who experience negative effects from that addiction.

> " Some people contend that online socialization . . . helps initiate real-world socialization. "

What Causes Online Addiction?

> **Internet addiction is based almost entirely off of a lack of willpower. My desire to browse the Internet is stronger than my desire to turn my computer off.**

—Lana Gorlinski, "Confessions of a Teenage Internet Addict," *Huffington Post*, July 2, 2013. www.huffingtonpost.com.

Gorlinski is a teenager from Orange County, California, who has struggled with the problem of spending too much time online.

....

> **Addiction appears to go deeper than just psychological dependence. There is emerging evidence indicating that, for example, our interaction with technology produces the same neurochemical reaction . . . found with alcohol, drug, sex, and gambling addictions.**

—Jim Taylor, "The Bad, the Ugly, and the Good of Children's Use of Social Media," *Huffington Post*, May 28, 2013. www.huffingtonpost.com.

Taylor is an adjunct professor at the University of San Francisco.

....

Bracketed quotes indicate conflicting positions.

* Editor's Note: While the definition of a primary source can be narrowly or broadly defined, for the purposes of Compact Research, a primary source consists of: 1) results of original research presented by an organization or researcher; 2) eyewitness accounts of events, personal experience, or work experience; 3) first-person editorials offering pundits' opinions; 4) government officials presenting political plans and/or policies; 5) representatives of organizations presenting testimony or policy.

66 In the present study, out of 1000 students . . . [s]ignificant usage differences were evident based on the gender of user. Males in comparison to females were significantly more likely to be addicted. 99

—Deepak Goel, Alka Subramanyam, and Ravinda Kamath, "A Study on the Prevalence of Internet Addiction and Its Association with Psychopathology in Indian Adolescents," *Indian Journal of Psychiatry*, April/June, 2013. www.indianjpsychiatry.org.

The authors are affiliated with the Department of Psychiatry at Topiwala National Medical College and B.Y.L. Nair Charitable Hospital in Mumbai, India.

66 [Our research study showed that] the gender split of those with problematic internet use versus those without was even, suggesting that typical views of internet addiction as a male problem are (certainly, now) unfounded. 99

—Michela Romano, Lisa A. Osborne, Roberto Truzoli, and Phil Reed, "Differential Psychological Impact of Internet Exposure on Internet Addicts," *PLOS ONE*, February 7, 2013. www.plosone.org.

Romano and Truzoli are affiliated with the University of Milan in Italy. Osborne and Reed are affiliated with Swansea University in the United Kingdom.

66 The current data . . . shows that there are clear indications for genetic causes of Internet addiction. 99

—Christian Montag, "Internet Addiction—Causes at the Molecular Level," EurekAlert!, press release, August 29, 2012. www.eurekalert.org.

Montag works in the Department for Differential and Biological Psychology at the University of Bonn in Germany.

66 College students are a group that may be particularly vulnerable to addiction, as they have largely unfettered, unsupervised access to the Internet and independent control of their time. 99

—Dimitri A. Christakis, Megan M. Moreno, Lauren Jelenchick, Mon T. Myaing, and Chuan Zhou, "Problematic Internet Usage in US College Students: A Pilot Study," *BMC Medicine*, June 22, 2011. www.biomedcentral.com.

The authors are from the Seattle Children's Research Institute, the Department of Pediatrics at the University of Washington, and the Department of Pediatrics at the University of Wisconsin.

❝[A] finding in our study is that parental SES [socioeconomic status] was inversely associated with adolescents' addictive Internet use. Parents of higher education attainment might be able to guide their children toward desirable Internet use and supervise children's Internet use effectively based on their knowledge of the Internet and its devices.❞

—Jongho Heo, Juhwan Oh, S.V. Subramanian, Yoon Kim, and Ichiro Kawachi, "Addictive Internet Use Among Korean Adolescents: A National Survey," *PLOS ONE*, February 5, 2014. www.plosone.org.

Jongho Heo is affiliated with the Public Health Joint Doctoral Program at San Diego State University and the University of California in San Diego. Juhwan Oh and Yoon Kim are affiliated with Seoul National University College of Medicine in Korea. S.V. Subramanian and Ichiro Kawachi work at the Harvard School of Public Health in Massachusetts.

❝This is a condition that is not defined by age, gender, ethnicity, income or level of education.❞

Dana Hinders, "What Causes Internet Addiction?," Livestrong.com. August 16, 2013.

Hinders is a journalist.

Facts and Illustrations

What Causes Online Addiction?

- In a study published in 2014 in *Addictive Behaviors* researchers studied **755 Chinese adolescents** and found that school, interpersonal, and anxiety problems were associated with a higher risk for Internet addiction.

- In a 2014 study in *Addiction Research & Theory* **319 participants** were studied, and researchers found that shyness was a significant predictor of gaming addiction.

- According to a 2013 study reported in *Research and Health*, compared to nonaddicted subjects, subjects with severe IAD had worse family functioning, higher neuroticism, and a history of more stressful life events.

- In a study published in 2012 in the *International Journal of Mental Health and Addiction*, researchers surveyed **438 players** of the online game *World of Warcraft* and found that **12 percent** believe that computer game addiction involves playing to alter or improve one's mood or to escape real world problems.

- A study of **1,022 university students**, published in 2014 in *Computers in Human Behavior*, shows that the ratio of male to female Internet addiction is 3 to 1.

- According to a study of **3,380 gamers** published in the *International Journal of Mental Health and Addiction* in 2014, males are more likely to be classified as problem gamers than females.

Five Traits That Drive Social Media Use

Some people have difficulty controlling their social media use and spend large amounts of time online—even to the point of exhibiting behavior that suggests addiction. Researchers have identified five psychological traits that commonly drive such use. These are expained below.

Trait	Description
Fear of Missing Out	The fear of missing out on important updates, news, or events causes many people to check their social networking sites frequently.
Ego	Research shows that people enjoy having an audience, and this drives them to make frequent postings.
Perceived Value	Many social media users believe that networking gives them numerous advantages and tools that they would not have otherwise—for example, instant access to breaking news or shopping deals.
Control	Social network users feel empowered because they have control over their experience, including what they access and when they do so.
Social Comparison/ Self-Esteem	Social networks allow people to compare themselves to others in order to assess their own strengths and weaknesses.

Source: Tom Lowery "Why Social Media Is So Addictive (And Why Marketers Should Care)," *CMS Wire*, August 28, 2013.

- In a 2014 study in the *International Journal of Mental Health and Addiction*, researchers analyzed data from **56,086 students** from four hundred middle schools and four hundred high schools and found that the prevalence of Internet addiction was higher in boys than in girls.

Mobile Phones Fuel Addiction

Many people believe Internet addiction is made worse by mobile phones because these devices provide a constant and easy connection to social networks and other websites. These graphs show that many people exhibit indications of addiction to their phones; a significant percentage check their phones frequently and feel that they cannot be without them for long periods of time. The graph is based on the results of a large survey of US adults.

How often do you check your mobile device?

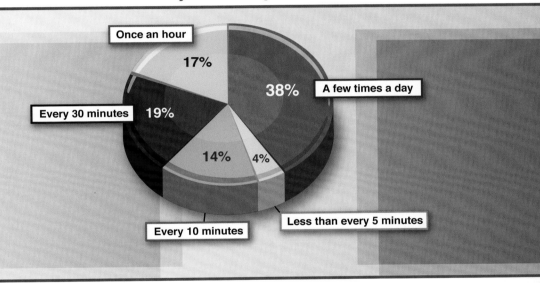

Once an hour 17%

Every 30 minutes 19%

A few times a day 38%

4% Less than every 5 minutes

14% Every 10 minutes

How long could you go without it?

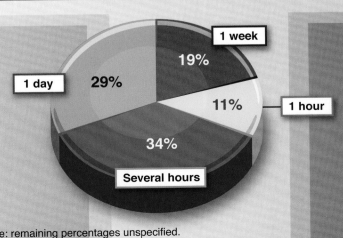

1 week 19%

1 day 29%

1 hour 11%

Several hours 34%

Note: remaining percentages unspecified.

Source: *Time*, "Your Wireless Life: Results of TIME's Mobility Poll," August 27, 2012. http://content.time.com.

- The website Internet Addiction Disorder estimates that Internet addicts are primarily younger than thirty years old; it says that approximately **35 percent** are under age nineteen, and **30 percent** are between nineteen and thirty years old.

- According to a 2013 research study of **3,105 adolescents** in the Netherlands, published in *Computers in Human Behavior*, every additional weekly hour spent playing online games increased the odds of being addicted to the Internet by **2.7 percent**.

- In 2012 *Time*, in cooperation with Qualcomm, polled close to five thousand people in eight countries and found that one in four people look at their phone every thirty minutes, and one in five, every five minutes. **Sixty-eight percent** place their phone next to their bed at night.

- In a 2013 poll of **2,252 US adults**, the Pew Research Center found that **56 percent** have smartphones.

- In a study published in 2014 in *Computers in Human Behavior*, researchers found that youth who were addicted to the Internet were more likely to have divorced parents, be an only child, and live with a single parent.

How Do Online Addictions Affect Health and Well-Being?

66The current incarnation of the Internet—portable, social, accelerated, and all-pervasive—may be making us not just dumber or lonelier but more depressed and anxious, prone to obsessive-compulsive and attention-deficit disorders, even outright psychotic.99

—Tony Dokoupil, journalist.

66For most people, the tie to the Internet, however powerful and consuming, brings much more pleasure or productivity than pain and impairment.99

—Allen Frances, professor emeritus at Duke University.

Twenty-eight-year-old Brett Walker started playing online games when he was eleven years old. He says that when he reached his early twenties he was addicted to the role-playing game *World of Warcraft*, playing for up to sixteen hours a day. While Walker says that he enjoyed his gameplay, as he spent increasing amounts of time online the rest of his life got progressively worse. "Whenever I was on the computer I would feel great," said Walker, "but whenever I'm lying in bed at night, I would always . . . just think about how that day I hadn't accomplished anything, about how I wasn't what I wanted to be in life and that I was really, you know, miserable."[40] As Walker's story reveals, online obsessions can have a profound impact on a person's health and well-being.

Brain Changes

Some research shows that when people use the Internet for large periods of time, the structure of their brains changes. For example, in a study published in 2011 researchers report that excessive Internet use seems to cause shrinkage in certain parts of the brain. The researchers used brain scans to examine the brains of Internet addicts and found that some areas—those thought to govern executive thinking skills, cognitive control, and emotional processing—were reduced by as much as 20 percent in some people. They theorize that this could result in behavioral changes, such as impaired inhibition or decision-making abilities.

> " Some research shows that when people use the Internet for large periods of time, the structure of their brains changes. "

However, while research does indicate that Internet use might change the brain, evidence about the meaning of such brain changes is lacking. In fact, the Internet is not unique in its ability to impact the structure of the brain; everything a person does and thinks about has an impact on the brain, which is constantly changing throughout life. Tom Stafford, lecturer in psychology and cognitive science at the University of Sheffield in the United Kingdom, explains, "Everything you do changes your brain. Everything. Every little thought or experience plays a role in the constant wiring and rewiring of your neural networks. So there is no escape. . . . Your life, however you live it, leaves traces in the brain."[41] As a result, some people argue, those brain changes are simply a normal part of life and not necessarily an indication of harm.

Physical Problems

People who spend large amounts of time online typically spend hours in one position such as sitting at a computer or holding a smartphone or other device. All this time in one position can cause numerous physical problems. Kevin Roberts describes the way that his hours of online gaming harmed him physically: "Those insane hours that I spent hunched over an inflexible computer chair during my last year at college wreaked havoc on my body. My lower back hurt. I ignored the discomfort. Soon I had pain shooting down my leg, which made walking difficult. The next part to suffer was my right wrist because of my constant use of a mouse. . . . I realized that game play was the culprit in all of these physical complaints. My screen time, nevertheless, continued unabated."[42] Reportedly, some people have died from blood clots that formed as a result of sitting at the computer for marathon sessions of gaming.

As Internet access via smartphone increases, new types of physical problems have arisen. For example, medical doctor Dean Fishman came up with the term "text neck" to describe the various ailments some people get from spending large amounts of time looking down at their smartphones. *CNN* writer Jacque Wilson explains the harms of this position: "Staying in what experts call the 'forward head posture' can lead to muscle strain, disc herniations and pinched nerves. Over time, it can even flatten or reverse the natural curve of your neck."[43]

Social Networking and Unhappiness

Some people believe that addiction to social networking websites causes unhappiness and depression. These sites amplify comparisons among people by displaying them for everyone to see. Chicago high school student Abby Abolt explains how this could cause unhappiness. She says, "It's like a big popularity contest—who can get the most friend requests or get the most pictures tagged." In her opinion, "If you really didn't have that many friends and weren't really doing much with your life, and saw other peoples' status updates and pictures and what they were doing with friends, I could see how that would make them upset."[44] Even a person who feels happy and secure can feel unhappy after seeing what

> " As Internet access via smartphone increases, new types of physical problems have arisen. "

other people are doing. Journalist Jenna Wortham explains how this happened to her: "One recent night, I curled up on my couch with popcorn and Netflix Instant, ready to spend a quiet night at home. The peace was sweet." However, she says, "Soon, my iPhone began flashing with notifications . . . about what my friends were doing." The result, "Suddenly, my simple domestic pleasures paled in comparison with the things I could be doing."[45]

Yet, while such anecdotes are common, research shows that most social network users are happy with their online experiences. For example, according to a 2012 report by Nielsen research company, 76 percent of people say they have positive feelings after participating in social media. A 2012 survey by Common Sense Media found that only 5 percent of teens believe that social networking makes them feel more depressed.

Constant Connection and Stress

Many people maintain an almost constant connection to their work and social networks, checking for messages all the time and responding immediately. However, the impact of this constant connection is unclear. Some people insist that while it differs from the past when people were not constantly on call to their friends and work colleagues, it is not harmful. Instead, they believe it is simply an evolution in how society communicates. Ira E. Hyman Jr., a professor of psychology at Western Washington University says, "Staying constantly in touch with your entire circle of friends may be the new norm. . . . To an outsider, they may appear addicted to their cell phones. But I see an emerging form of social interaction."[46] However, critics contend that constant connection is inherently stressful. Columnist Beth Kassab explains, "People aren't wired to be in a constant state of alertness. That keeps levels of stress hormones high and might eventually hurt how well you sleep or even take a toll on your heart."[47]

> " Most social network users are happy with their online experiences. "

Personal Relationships

Spending large amounts of time online can have a negative impact on one's personal relationships. To some people, the Internet becomes the single most important thing in their lives, and they ignore relationships with friends and family. Addiction specialist Hilarie Cash explains, "Because they are neglecting the real world . . . things fall apart. It's like a heroin addict who goes on a heroin binge, and just wants to be in that cave. They completely forget about the world. If they are married and have kids, they're not taking care of them. If they are students, they're not taking care of academics."[48]

However, while some people neglect important personal relationships because of the Internet, other people who spend large amounts of time online actually strengthen their personal relationships in the process. For example, social networking is an intensely social activity. In addition, many gamers develop numerous new friendships because they play with other people online. Michael Friedman, professor at Columbia University Schools of Social Work and Public Health, argues that overall the Internet has a positive impact on most people's relationships. He says, "Let's be very careful about indicting . . . new technology that undoubtedly has its risks but also has great benefits." In his opinion, "Certainly some of this Internet use is problematic. . . . But it also makes it possible to be more efficient and effective, to be better informed, to participate in political life easily, and to have relationships that would otherwise be impossible due to constraints of time and distance."[49]

> "Spending large amounts of time online can have a negative impact on one's personal relationships."

Social Development in Youth

Some people engage in almost all their communication online rather than in person; for example, communicating with friends through social networking sites. Critics worry that this is extremely harmful to youth because they are not developing important social skills that can be learned only through face-to-face communication. Melissa Ortega is a child psychologist at the Child Mind Institute in New York. She frequently sees youth who lack basic face-to-face communication skills because they do not practice them enough. For example, she says, "They may have trouble initiating interactions, those small talk situations. They don't have as much experience doing it because they're not engaging in it

> Social networking is an intensely social activity.

ever."[50] Ortega worries about how this inability to talk to people will harm young people later in life.

Researcher danah boyd has spent years interviewing youth across the United States, and she contends this lack of face-to-face interaction is not caused by an addiction to communicating through the Internet. Instead, she argues that youth increasingly rely on the Internet for communication simply because they have no other way to socialize with one another. She explains, "The reason technology plays such a powerful role for them is that it's how they can just get together." She argues that various social changes, such as people living farther apart from one another, have made it more difficult for youth to hang out in person. She says, "[The Internet] has become the primary place where young people can hang out with their peers. Kids want to be on these sites because that's where their friends are. That's the whole thing."[51]

A Lack of Research

While critics raise all kinds of fears about the harms of Internet addiction, some researchers insist that these fears are not justified because they are not supported by research. They argue that spending large amounts of time online is a recent phenomenon and that more time and research is needed to really understand how this will impact society. Dan Becker, adolescent psychiatrist and medical director of Mills-Peninsula's Behavioral Health Services program, discusses Internet use in youth. He points out that never before in history have youth spent so much time using the Internet, and he argues that there is simply no way to know for sure what the future effects of this behavior will be. He says, "So much is changing so quickly in how people behave in our culture. We haven't had enough time to see what happens later in life to kids who spend extensive time with electronic media. We aren't going to know whether there will be negative long-term effects until these kids have their own kids."[52]

Overall, people disagree about the effects of spending large amounts of time online. Critics warn that the Internet can cause serious harm to both mind and body, yet others caution that society should not be so quick to condemn this technology because it also offers many unique benefits.

Primary Source Quotes*

How Do Online Addictions Affect Health and Well-Being?

" We can put to bed the question of whether people feel the Internet brings them together or isolates them: This survey tells us that most connected users in the US believe the Web has strengthened their relationships. "

—Tim Berners-Lee, "Statement from Sir Tim Berners-Lee on the 25th Anniversary of the Web," Pew Research Internet Project, March 11, 2014. www.pewinternet.org.

Berners-Lee invented the World Wide Web in 1989.

" A characteristic 21st-century American . . . [is] more electronically networked but more personally isolated than ever before. "

—Ross Douthat, "The Man with the Google Glasses," *New York Times*, April 14, 2012. www.nytimes.com.

Douthat is a columnist for the *New York Times*.

Bracketed quotes indicate conflicting positions.

* Editor's Note: While the definition of a primary source can be narrowly or broadly defined, for the purposes of Compact Research, a primary source consists of: 1) results of original research presented by an organization or researcher; 2) eyewitness accounts of events, personal experience, or work experience; 3) first-person editorials offering pundits' opinions; 4) government officials presenting political plans and/or policies; 5) representatives of organizations presenting testimony or policy.

66 **Engaging in various forms of social media is a routine activity that research has shown to benefit children and adolescents by enhancing communication, social connection, and even technical skills.** 99

—Gwenn Schurgin O'Keeffe, Kathleen Clarke-Pearson, and Council on Families, "Clinical Report: The Impact of Social Media on Children, Adolescents, and Families," *Pediatrics*, March 28, 2011. http://pediatrics.aappublications.org.

O'Keeffe is a pediatrician, author, and health journalist, and Clarke-Pearson is a pediatrician. The Council on Communications and Media is an organization dedicated to advancing children's health.

66 **There is a dark side to . . . [Facebook] use, along with other forms of social media, that has been labeled Facebook Depression, though this phenomenon also includes anxiety, other psychiatric disorders, and a range of unhealthy behaviors.** 99

—Jim Taylor, "The Bad, the Ugly, and the Good of Children's Use of Social Media," *Huffington Post*, May 28, 2013. www.huffingtonpost.com.

Taylor is an adjunct professor at the University of San Francisco.

66 **Our dependence on technology and our inability to be away from it for even a few minutes is just one clear indicator that we are not functioning at our best level. If our minds are always worrying about what we are missing then how can we focus attention on what we are getting?** 99

—Larry D. Rosen, with Nancy A. Cheever and L. Mark Carrier, *iDisorder: Understanding Our Obsession with Technology and Overcoming Its Hold on Us*. New York: Palgrave Macmillan, 2012, p. 15.

Rosen is past chair and professor of psychology at California State University, Dominguez Hills. He is a research psychologist and a computer educator. Cheever is associate professor and chair of Communication, and L. Mark Carrier is professor and chair of Psychology at California State University, Dominguez Hills.

66 **There is a significant positive correlation between levels of depression and internet addiction.** 99

—Ozgul Orsal, Ozlem Orsal, Alaettin Unsal, and S. Sinan Ozalp, "Evaluation of Internet Addiction and Depression among University Students," *Procedia —Social and Behavioral Sciences*, July 2013. www.sciencedirect.com.

The authors are affiliated with Eskisehir Osmangazi University in Turkey.

66 **Current research regarding the impact of Internet use on mental health and human life is inconclusive.** 99

—Michael Friedman, "Internet Addiction: A Public Health Crisis?," *Huffington Post*, April 22, 2011. www.huffingtonpost.com.

Friedman is a professor at the Columbia University Schools of Social Work and Public Health.

66 **Because people can typically be found with their cell phones within reach, friends, family, and employers expect immediate responses. . . . Increasing numbers of people are experiencing anxiety over this constant deluge of messages and notifications and the demands these place on people's attention and time.** 99

—Pacific Quest, "The Internet Age & Rise of Smartphones," Internet Addiction Resource, October 1, 2013. http://internetaddictionresource.com.

Pacific Quest is an addiction recovery program.

66 **Academic problems caused by Internet addiction include decline in study habits, significant drop in grades, missing classes, increased risk of being placed on academic probation, and poor integration in extra-curricular activities.** 99

—Noreen Akhter, "Relationship Between Internet Addiction and Academic Performance among University Undergraduates," *Educational Research and Reviews, Academic Journals,* July 18, 2013. http://academicjournals.org.

Akhter works at the National University of Sciences and Technology in Islamabad, Pakistan.

66 **Using technology for such prolonged periods also means that addicts aren't getting the proper exercise, sometimes leaving addicts at increased risk for back strain, carpal tunnel syndrome, and other medical conditions.** 99

—Bradford Regional Medical Center, "Internet Addiction Treatment and Recovery Program, a Patient and Family Guide," 2013. www.brmc.com.

The Bradford Regional Medical Center created one of the first inpatient Internet addiction treatment centers in the United States.

How Do Online Addictions Affect Health and Well-Being?

- In a study published in 2014 in *Psychiatry Research*, study subjects who were addicted to the Internet scored higher for depression and anxiety and lower for self-directedness and cooperativeness.

- In a study of thirty males addicted to the Internet and thirty who are not addicted to the Internet, researchers report in a 2014 issue of *General Hospital Psychiatry* that those addicted to the Internet believe their family functioning is more negative than those who are not addicted.

- In a study published in 2013 in the journal *PLOS ONE*, researchers had sixty volunteers spend fifteen minutes online, then tested their mood and anxiety levels. Those volunteers who had reported that they were addicted to the Internet showed increased negative moods after being online than those who did not report addiction.

- According to a 2012 survey of **802 teens** by the Pew Research Center, **52 percent** of online teens say they have had an experience online that made them feel good about themselves.

- The Pew Research Center reports that according to a 2014 survey of **1,006 adults, 67 percent** of Internet users say their online communication with family and friends has generally strengthened those relationships, while **18 percent** say it generally weakens those relationships.

Most People Believe the Internet Is Beneficial

Although some people show signs of being addicted to the Internet, polls show that overall most people believe the Internet benefits society. This graph shows the results of a poll of 1,006 US adults aged eighteen and over. A large majority of respondents describe the Internet as good for society and for themselves as individuals.

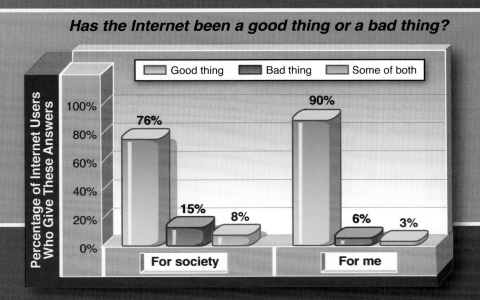

Has the Internet been a good thing or a bad thing?

Source: Pew Research Center, "The Web at 25 in the U.S.: The Overall Verdict: The Internet Has Been a Plus for Society and an Especially Good Thing for Individual Users," February 27, 2014. www.pewinternet.org.

- In a study reported in the *Journal of Adolescence* in 2014, researchers found that **24.2 percent** of surveyed students were moderate or serious overusers of the Internet; however, these students did not report any harm caused by their Internet use.

- In a study published in 2014 in *Computers in Human Behavior*, youth who were addicted to the Internet viewed their parents as less supportive and more punitive than youth who were not addicted.

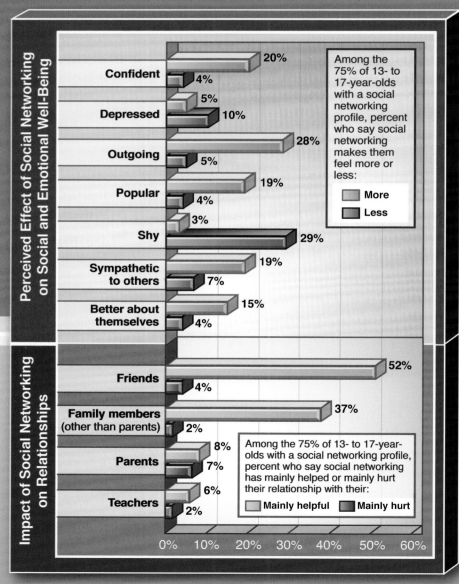

Teens Say Social Networking Is a Positive Experience

Most US teens believe that social networking has a positive impact on their relationships and on their social and emotional well-being. The majority of 1,030 teenagers surveyed described social networking as helping their relationships with friends and family. They also said social networking makes them feel more confident and outgoing.

Perceived Effect of Social Networking on Social and Emotional Well-Being

Confident — 20% / 4%
Depressed — 5% / 10%
Outgoing — 28% / 5%
Popular — 19% / 4%
Shy — 3% / 29%
Sympathetic to others — 19% / 7%
Better about themselves — 15% / 4%

Among the 75% of 13- to 17-year-olds with a social networking profile, percent who say social networking makes them feel more or less:

■ More
■ Less

Impact of Social Networking on Relationships

Friends — 52% / 4%
Family members (other than parents) — 37% / 2%
Parents — 8% / 7%
Teachers — 6% / 2%

Among the 75% of 13- to 17-year-olds with a social networking profile, percent who say social networking has mainly helped or mainly hurt their relationship with their:

■ Mainly helpful   ■ Mainly hurt

0% 10% 20% 30% 40% 50% 60%

Source: Common Sense Media, "Social Media, Social Life: How Teens View Their Digital Lives," Summer 2012. www.commonsensemedia.com.

Internet Addicts Exhibit Anxiety and Depression

Researchers in India evaluated the mental and physical health of college-age Internet users in Mumbai. Using a test to determine Internet addiction, participants were classified as moderate or average users, possible addicts, or addicts (meaning those who reported excessive Internet use). Although addicts represented the smallest of the three groups, their health profile revealed high levels of anxiety and depression. In the chart below, higher scores represent better health. The scores are based on questionnaires completed by each participant.

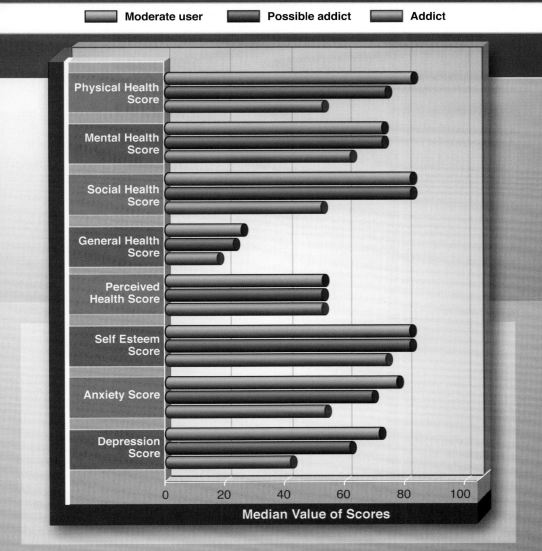

Source: Deepak Goel, Alka Subramanyam, and Ravindra Kamath, "A Study on the Prevalence of Internet Addiction and Its Association with Psychopathology in Indian Adolescents," *Indian Journal of Psychiatry*, April/June, 2013. www.ncbi.nlm.nih.gov.

Many People Worry About Reliance on the Internet

This graph shows the results of a survey of 7,219 adults in nineteen countries. A significant percentage of those surveyed expressed concern over their addiction to, or overreliance on, the Internet and other digital technology. They were concerned that this technology interferes with family life, impairs their ability to focus, and distracts them too often.

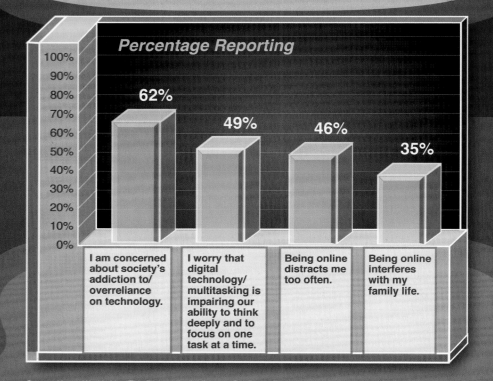

Percentage Reporting

62%	**49%**	**46%**	**35%**
I am concerned about society's addiction to/ overreliance on technology.	I worry that digital technology/ multitasking is impairing our ability to think deeply and to focus on one task at a time.	Being online distracts me too often.	Being online interferes with my family life.

Source: Havas Worldwide, "This Digital Life: Addicted to Our Digital Tools," vol. 13, 2012. www.prosumer-report.com.

- According to a 2013 report by *Business Week*, when people have e-mail open constantly at work, they switch tasks an average of **37 times** every hour.

- In a study published in 2010 in *Computers in Human Behavior*, researchers studied **219 university students** and found that Facebook users spent less time studying and had lower grade point averages than students who did not use Facebook.

How Can People Overcome Internet and Social Media Addiction?

> 66 The most basic way to curb addictive gaming habits is to simply stop playing. The same can be said for any other internet use or abuse. 99
>
> —Pacific Quest, an addiction recovery program.

> 66 There is much more to full recovery than simply refraining from the Internet. Complete recovery means addressing the underlying issues that led up to the behavior. 99
>
> —Kimberly S. Young, Internet addiction researcher, and Cristiano Nabuco de Abreu, director of the Integrated Impulse Disorders Outpatient Unit at the University of São Paulo, Brazil.

Screen-Free Week is a yearly event that began in 1994. During one week in May people are encouraged to refrain from using screen media—including the Internet—unless that use is required for work. Campaign for a Commercial-Free Childhood, which organizes the event, argues that screen media dominates the lives of far too many people. It says, "Screen-Free Week is a fun and innovative opportunity to reduce our dependence on entertainment screen media. . . . It's a chance for children—and adults—to rediscover the joys of life beyond the screen."[53] While the possibility of becoming addicted to the Internet is still debated, those who do believe addiction is possible have suggested numerous ways to help reduce Internet and social media addiction. Reducing screen time is just one approach that has been suggested.

Setting Limits

Most experts agree that setting limits on one's Internet use is an important part of overcoming Internet addiction. People accomplish this in a number of different ways; for example, one strategy is to take breaks from the Internet throughout the day. Even computer programs can help with this; for instance, a program called *Freedom* can disable Internet access on users' computers for a set amount of time. The Internet can be accessed only after that amount of time has passed or when users reboot their computers. Other people set limits by creating Internet-free areas of their homes or Internet-free times of day. For instance, television host Ari Melber says that he and his fiancé have a digital curfew: no screen time after 11 p.m. Melber says they instituted this rule after a vacation during which they did not have Internet access and realized that this was actually beneficial. He says that without the Internet, "We found the evenings more relaxing, and we were sleeping better."[54] Another rule that is becoming common is to ban cell phones from the bedroom. This allows users to relax and sleep without the temptation of constantly checking messages and accessing the Internet.

> **Most experts agree that setting limits on one's Internet use is an important part of overcoming Internet addiction.**

Education

Some people insist that the best way to address the problem of Internet and social media addiction is to prevent it from developing in the first place. This means educating people about the Internet from a young age and teaching them about the dangers of addiction and how to avoid it. Writer Whitney Mallett believes South Korea provides a good example of how such education can be accomplished. She says, "The Ministry of Public Administration and Security is making the dangers of Internet addiction a mandatory part of the curriculum from preschool to high school. This seems like a preventative measure that could limit how many youth might otherwise eventually need to attend . . . [a treatment] program."[55]

While South Korea and a few other countries have taken such preventative action, most nations have not. Critics argue that due to this general lack of education, most people use the Internet without even thinking about how it is affecting them. Tony Dokoupil explains, "All of us, since the relationship with the Internet began, have tended to accept it as is, without much conscious thought about how we want it to be or what we want to avoid." He argues that rather than simply allowing the Internet to shape their lives in this way, people should consciously think about what they want or do not want from their Internet use, then make that happen. He says, "Those days of complacency should end. The Internet is still ours to shape. Our minds are in the balance."[56]

Managing Use

Many addiction treatment specialists argue that since participating in society is difficult without using the Internet, learning how to manage its use is the best way for people to overcome addiction to it. This differs from treatment for some other types of addiction, which teach addicts to avoid whatever they are addicted to. For example, alcoholics try to avoid exposure to alcohol and situations in which they will be tempted to drink it. Cosette Dawna Rae, who works at the reSTART Internet addiction treatment center, discusses how difficult it is to avoid the Internet. She says, "People here tell me, 'Cosette, we think this is the hardest addiction to break, more than any chemical, because it's free, legal, accessible, everywhere and everybody's doing it.'"[57]

> **Participating in society is difficult without using the Internet.**

Hilarie Cash says that people need to figure out how to safely use the Internet by identifying the elements that pose a threat to them. She says, "They can define what are those aspects of Internet use that are problems for them and be abstinent from those and then define for themselves how they're going to use computers and the Internet in a way that is healthy and sustaining."[58]

Increasing the Number of Addiction Treatment Centers

Some people believe that in order to successfully combat the problem of Internet addiction, the United States needs far more treatment centers, including inpatient treatment centers. Psychologist Kimberly Young, an Internet addiction specialist and founder of the Center for Internet Addiction, insists, "We're really behind other countries in treating this problem." She says, "China, Korea and Taiwan all have treatment centers. Here in the United States, people who need treatment don't have anywhere to go."[59] It is true that the United States has a limited number of treatment facilities dedicated to Internet addiction. However, critics question the usefulness of such centers. Rebecca J. Rosen, a senior editor at the *Atlantic*, reviewed a number of studies on treatment programs and concludes, "Do these programs work? So far there isn't much evidence to support them." According to Rosen, the problem is that Internet addiction has a huge variety of causes. She says, "Patients at these centers could be suffering from a range of problems—anything from pathological gambling (which can certainly manifest itself online) to sleep disorders and depression."[60] Critics like Rosen argue that rather than being treated in a facility focused on Internet addiction, these people would benefit more from a program targeting the real causes of that addiction.

> " The United States has a limited number of treatment facilities dedicated to Internet addiction. "

Cognitive Behavioral Therapy

Some therapists treat Internet addiction with cognitive behavioral therapy (CBT), a type of psychotherapy that helps people replace harmful thoughts and behavior patterns with healthier ones. With this treatment patients are taught to identify the thoughts that trigger addictive feelings and actions and modify their behavior to avoid these triggers. Therapists have found that some people use the Internet excessively in order to cope with uncomfortable emotions such as stress or anxiety, so CBT includes learning other ways to cope with these emotions. CBT is successfully used by therapists to treat other types of disorders, such as substance abuse and eating disorders. Young uses CBT to treat her patients and states that this type of treatment generally lasts three months and is very effective for IAD.

Addressing Underlying Problems

Some people believe Internet addiction is simply a case of bad behavior and a lack of discipline, and that to overcome it individuals must learn to exercise self-control over their Internet use. Many treatment facilities in China incorporate this idea in their treatment methods. Patients at military-style boot camps there are subject to strict routines and harsh discipline to help restore their sense of self-control.

However, others contend that Internet addiction is actually the result of deeper underlying problems, such as depression, and insist that to successfully treat it, those problems must be addressed. According to a publication by the Internet Addiction Treatment and Recovery Program at the Bradford Regional Medical Center in Pennsylvania, "Internet addiction stems from other emotional or situational problems, including depression, anxiety, stress, relationship troubles, academic difficulties, impulse control problems, and sexual abuse."[61] As a result, the center advises that treatment must include addressing those underlying problems or addiction relapses will occur.

> " Some people believe Internet addiction is simply a case of bad behavior and a lack of discipline. "

Boot Camps

Some Asian nations use military-style boot camps to treat Internet addiction; however, the effectiveness of these is controversial. To make the 2014 documentary *Web Junkie*, Shosh Shlam and Hilla Medalia went to one of China's Internet addiction treatment centers and found that while treatment methods such as intense boot-camp-style exercise are extremely harsh, there are some indications of effectiveness. For example, they state that the Daxing Boot Camp near Beijing, where they filmed, claims a 70 percent success rate. They conclude, "If that's true, perhaps

China's treatment model is something other nations should embrace, however disturbing it may seem to outsiders."[62]

However, at the same time, the filmmakers remain unsure about the effectiveness of this treatment. They say, "After four months of filming in this center . . . some vital questions remained: Are the children being accurately evaluated? And is the treatment effective? In many cases, it seemed parents were blaming the Internet for complex social and behavioral issues that may defy such interventions. (For example, we noticed that some patients experienced difficult family relationships, social introversion and a lack of friends in the physical world.)"[63] The filmmakers are not alone with their questions. These camps have been subject to extensive criticism regarding their effectiveness and safety, especially following the deaths of some youth undergoing treatment. For instance, in 2009 counselors at Qihang Salvation Training Camp in rural China reportedly beat to death Deng Sanshan, who was being treated for video game and Internet addiction.

> " Internet addiction is not a medically recognized disorder in the United States, so it is not covered by insurance. "

Formal Recognition of Internet Addiction as a Medical Disorder

Some people argue that formally recognizing Internet addiction as a medical disorder is the best way to help addicts. At present, Internet addiction is not a medically recognized disorder in the United States, so treatment is not covered by insurance. As a result, it is generally very expensive for addicts to obtain professional assistance. For instance, according to news reports, the reSTART treatment program near Washington costs $22,000 for a forty-five-day stay. Treatment at the inpatient addiction treatment center at the Bradford Regional Medical Center in Pennsylvania is reported to be $14,000. For the majority of the population, such costs make this type of treatment impossible. However, if Internet addiction were classified as an official disorder, sufferers would be able to receive insurance coverage for their treatment, making treatment more attainable for many more people.

On the other hand, critics contend that classifying Internet addiction as an official disorder will actually make it more difficult for addicts to receive proper treatment. They argue that Internet addiction is really a side-effect of various other problems, and calling it a disorder will confuse the issue and take focus away from the real problems that are causing this behavior. Psychoanalyst Todd Essig says, "The fact of the matter is that when someone is suffering . . . they will use whatever is at hand to make the hurt go away." He warns, "If we ignore why someone spends their life playing *World of Warcraft*, cruising sex sites, or chatting online with strangers and we focus too much on the 'addiction' we will lose the chance to help."[64]

In the United States and around the world, an increasing number of people believe that Internet and social media addiction is a serious problem for a significant number of people. However there is much less agreement over what to do about it. Researchers, medical professionals, and the general public continue to struggle to understand why these addictions occur and what the best way is to prevent them and treat them.

Primary Source Quotes*

How Can People Overcome Internet and Social Media Addiction?

66 We support the development of uniform diagnostic criteria and the inclusion of IAD [Internet Addiction Disorder] in the DSM-V [Diagnostic and Statistical Manual of Mental Disorders] in order to advance public education, diagnosis and treatment of this important disorder. 99

—Hilarie Cash, Cosette D. Rae, Anne H. Steel, and Alexander Winkler, "Internet Addiction: A Brief Summary of Research and Practice," *Current Psychiatry Reviews*, vol. 8, no. 4, 2012, p. 292.

Cash, Rae, and Steel work at reSTART, an Internet addiction recovery program in Fall City, Washington. Winkler works in the Department for Clinical Psychology and Psychotherapy at the University of Marburg, Germany.

66 Making 'Internet addiction' an official diagnostic category is just wrong on so many levels, including, I believe, making it more difficult to get the right kind of help to those who have actually become painfully stuck online. 99

—Todd Essig, "Over-Stimulated: Staying Human in a Post-Human World," *Psychology Today*, February 15, 2010. www.psychologytoday.com.

Essig is a psychoanalyst.

Bracketed quotes indicate conflicting positions.

* Editor's Note: While the definition of a primary source can be narrowly or broadly defined, for the purposes of Compact Research, a primary source consists of: 1) results of original research presented by an organization or researcher; 2) eyewitness accounts of events, personal experience, or work experience; 3) first-person editorials offering pundits' opinions; 4) government officials presenting political plans and/or policies; 5) representatives of organizations presenting testimony or policy.

Primary Source Quotes

❝Do I believe that inpatient care is necessary for Internet addiction? Yes. . . . Inpatient care is necessary!❞

—Kimberly Young, "Inpatient Care for Internet Addiction: Is It Necessary?" Center for Internet Addiction, October 3, 2013. http://netaddictionrecovery.blogspot.com.

Young is a well-known Internet addiction researcher. She is author of *Caught in the Net* and founded the Center for Internet Addiction.

❝What is becoming more obvious to experts is the fact that addictions of any kind aren't helped much by inpatient treatment, except in the most life-threatening cases. And for the most part, the pull of the internet doesn't qualify for such measures.❞

—Maia Szalavitz, "Addicted to the Internet? There's a Hospital-Based Treatment for That," *Time*, September 5, 2013. http://healthland.time.com.

Szalavitz is a neuroscience journalist for *Time* magazine and coauthor of *Born for Love: Why Empathy Is Essential—and Endangered*.

❝For some people, the only way to minimize . . . [the harmful effects of social media] is to go cold turkey. That's the route I've taken, with Facebook.❞

—Michael W. Austin, "Facebook Addiction?" *Psychology Today*, February 20, 2012. www.psychologytoday.com.

Austin is a professor of philosophy at Eastern Kentucky University. He has published numerous books and journal articles related to ethics, philosophy of religion, philosophy of the family, and philosophy of sport.

❝Addicts falsely assume that just stopping the behavior is enough to say, 'I am recovered.' . . . Complete recovery means investigating the underlying issues that led up to the behavior and resolving them in a healthy manner.❞

—Bradford Regional Medical Center, "Internet Addiction Treatment and Recovery Program, A Patient and Family Guide," 2013. www.brmc.com.

The Internet Addiction Treatment and Recovery Program at the Bradford Regional Medical Center in Pennsylvania opened in 2013. It is the first inpatient treatment program for Internet addiction in the United States.

❝From the literature analysis we observed that CBT [cognitive behavioral therapy] is the most effective treatment for IAD [Internet Addiction Disorder].❞

—Fatima Shad Kaneez, Kejing Zhu, Liming Tie, and Nurul Bahriah Haji Osman, "Is Cognitive Behavioral Therapy an Intervention for Possible Internet Addiction Disorder?" *Journal of Drug and Alcohol Research*, vol. 2, 2013. www.ashdin.com.

The authors are affiliated with the University Brunei Darussalam in Brunei.

❝There's some research on . . . [Internet addiction], but we need more, and it needs to be taken more seriously than it currently is.❞

—Patrik Wincent, interview by Caisa Ederyd, "The Man Who Wants to Cure Your Internet Addiction," *Vice*, February 18, 2014. www.vice.com.

Wincent is a licensed therapist and founder of an Internet addiction treatment center in Sweden.

How Can People Overcome Internet and Social Media Addiction?

- In a 2014 survey of **1,006 people** by the Pew Research Center, about four in ten said they absolutely need to have Internet access for job-related or other reasons.

- The reSTART Internet addiction recovery treatment center in Washington reports that the completion rate for its program is **94 percent**.

- According to a report by the *New York Times*, due to counseling programs and other government efforts, between 2007 and 2009 the number of teenagers with symptoms of Internet addiction in South Korea decreased from more than a million to **938,000**.

- According to a 2014 study in the *International Journal of Mental Health and Addiction,* when data from **56,086 students** from four hundred middle schools and four hundred high schools were analyzed, researchers found that girls with emotional difficulties such as subjective unhappiness or depressive symptoms had much higher risks of Internet addiction than did boys with similar problems. Researchers concluded that more attention should be given to developing Internet addiction prevention programs tailored to fit boys' and girls' different needs.

- According to a survey of more than seven thousand people around the world by Havas Worldwide, more than **50 percent** of those surveyed say they enjoy deliberately taking breaks from their phones and mobile devices.

Addiction Treatment Shows Success

Some people believe inpatient treatment at a specialized addiction treatment facility is an effective way to combat Internet addiction. This graph shows the outcome of patient treatment within a one-year period at the reSTART Internet Addiction Recovery Program in Washington.

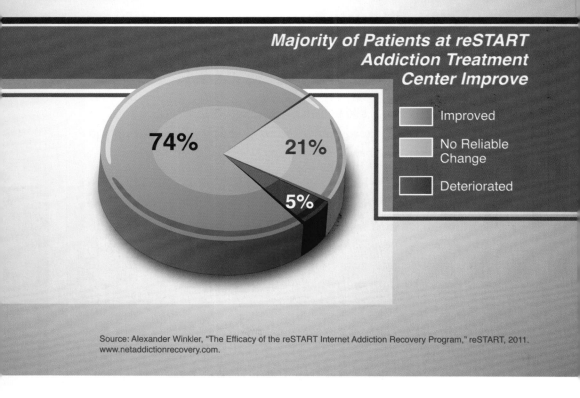

Majority of Patients at reSTART Addiction Treatment Center Improve

74%

21%

5%

- Improved
- No Reliable Change
- Deteriorated

Source: Alexander Winkler, "The Efficacy of the reSTART Internet Addiction Recovery Program," reSTART, 2011. www.netaddictionrecovery.com.

- According to a 2012 report by the Boston Consulting Group, the Internet is a vital part of the United States economy; its contribution to the gross domestic product exceeds that of the federal government.

- According to the reSTART Internet addiction recovery treatment center, between 2012 and 2013, **5 percent** of its patients left the program against medical advice.

Cognitive Behavior Therapy Has Proved Effective

This chart summarizes the results of a number of studies involving cognitive behavioral theraphy for treating internet addiction. It reveals that in each case, there were indications of the success of this therapy, including reductions in symptoms and an increase in the ability of patients to manage their symptoms.

Exhibited Outcomes of Cognitive Behavioral Therapy for Internet Addiction Disorder (IAD)

Year	Country	Participants	Intervention Outcomes
2001	United States	An 18-year-old female Internet-addicted college student.	Decrease in the level of self criticism and personal isolation, increase in cognition.
2007	United States	114 IAD clients from the Center for Online Addiction were recruited; 66 were males and 48 were females.	Most clients were able to manage their symptoms by the eighth session.The effect of self-management was sustained when a six-month follow-up was performed.
2010	China	56 IAD adolescents (12 to 17 years-old) were recruited from secondary school.	Improved time management skills and better emotional, cognitive, and behavioral symptoms.
2010	Greece	40 teenage boys (mean age 15 years) identified as IAD patients and recruited from a specialized outpatient unit for Internet and PC addiction.	During the first year of operations the unit treated a variety of IAD cases with success.
2011	China	38 IAD patients (aged 25 to 34 years) and 48 non-IAD volunteers (aged 25–33 years) as controls.	Results after three months of therapy indicate significant increase in attention and cognition.

Source: Fatima Shad Kaneez et al., "Is Cognitive Behavioral Therapy an Intervention for Possible Internet Addiction Disorder?," *Journal of Drug and Alcohol Research*, vol. 2, 2013. www.ashdin.com.

The Challenges of Unplugging

One common piece of advice for people who feel they are becoming addicted to social media and the Internet is to take regular breaks, or unplug, periodically. In an effort to determine the effects of unplugging, a group of researchers asked about one thousand college students from ten countries to abstain from using all electronoic media devices for twenty-four hours. At the end of that period, the students were asked to describe their successes and failures as well as their overal feelings about being unplugged. While a significant percentage reported that unplugging for a day was beneficial, many said the experiment left them feeling addicted, distressed, confused, or isolated. Some even described their attempt to abstain from electronic media as a failure.

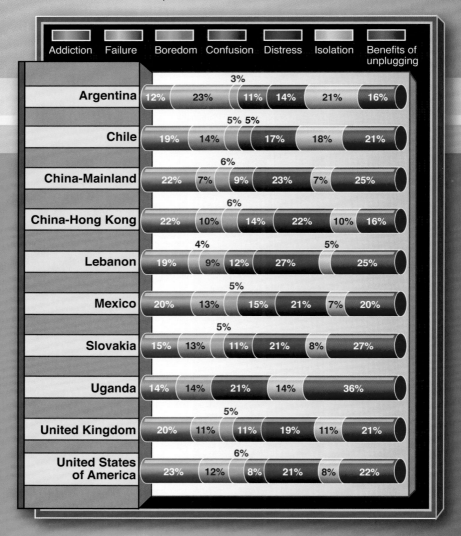

	Addiction	Failure	Boredom	Confusion	Distress	Isolation	Benefits of unplugging
Argentina	12%	23%	3% / 11%	14%	21%		16%
Chile	19%	14%	5% 5%	17%	18%		21%
China-Mainland	22%	7%	6% / 9%	23%	7%		25%
China-Hong Kong	22%	10%	6% / 14%	22%	10%		16%
Lebanon	19%	9%	4% / 12%	27%	5%		25%
Mexico	20%	13%	5% / 15%	21%	7%		20%
Slovakia	15%	13%	5% / 11%	21%	8%		27%
Uganda	14%	14%	21%	14%			36%
United Kingdom	20%	11%	5% / 11%	19%	11%		21%
United States of America	23%	12%	6% / 8%	21%	8%		22%

Source: International Center for Media & the Public Agenda, University of Maryland, "The World Unplugged: Reactions by Emotional Type," 2011. http://theworldunplugged.files.wordpress.com.

- The Center for Internet Addiction estimates that **70 percent** of Internet addicts also suffer from other addictions, including drugs, alcohol, and smoking.

- In 2010 the Kaiser Family Foundation reported that children aged eight to eighteen spend an average of **11 hours** consuming media, including the Internet, every day.

- In a 2012 survey of approximately five thousand people, *Time* magazine and Qualcomm found that **29 percent** of respondents fear that society places too much emphasis on technology such as the Internet.

- In a study published in 2010 in *Experimental and Clinical Psychopharmacology*, researchers reported that when subjects were treated with an antidepressant medication, there was a decrease in cravings for Internet video game play and a decrease in total game play time.

Key People and Advocacy Groups

Elias Aboujaoude: Aboujaoude is a psychiatrist and addiction expert. He is director of the Impulse Control Disorders Clinic at Stanford University School of Medicine and author of numerous publications on Internet addiction.

American Psychiatric Association (APA): The APA is the world's largest professional psychiatric organization and the publisher of the *DSM*.

Hilarie Cash: Cash is a psychiatrist and cofounder of reSTART, the first inpatient online addiction recovery program in the United States.

Center for Internet Addiction: The Center for Internet Addiction was founded by psychologist Kimberly S. Young in 1995 to help people who are addicted to the Internet.

Allen Frances: Allen Frances is a psychiatrist and professor emeritus at Duke University in North Carolina. He was chairman of the APA's fourth edition of the *DSM*, published in 2000.

Ivan Goldberg: Goldberg is a psychiatrist who created the term "internet addiction disorder" in 1995 as a joke on his colleagues.

David Greenfield: Greenfield is a psychologist and founder of the Center for Internet and Technology Addiction in West Hartford, Connecticut.

Mark D. Griffiths: Griffiths is an English psychologist and an expert in the field of gaming addiction. He is the director of the International Gaming Research Unit, which researches the psychosocial factors related to gaming.

Cosette Dawna Rae: Rae is a psychotherapist and cofounder of re-START, the first inpatient online addiction recovery program in the United States.

Kimberly Young: Kimberly Young is a psychologist and Internet addiction expert. She founded one of the first inpatient treatment programs for addiction to the Internet, which opened in 2013 at Bradford Regional Medical Center in Pennsylvania.

Chronology

1973
Empire, the first networked multiplayer game, is created. This spacecraft war game is a precursor to the hugely popular massively multiplayer online role-playing games (MMORPGs) that some people play for hours a day.

1989
British scientist Tim Berners-Lee writes the proposal for what will become the World Wide Web.

1999
Psychologist David Greenfield founds the Center for Internet and Technology Addiction in West Hartford, Connecticut.

1970   **1990**   **2000**

1992
IBM develops the Simon Personal Communicator—the first smartphone able to send and receive calls, faxes, and e-mails and have a touch-screen display. This device was a precursor to today's smartphones, which allow easy access to the Internet and social networking sites.

1996
Kimberly Young presents the first study on Internet addiction at the American Psychological Association's annual conference in Toronto. Her study is titled "Internet Addiction: The Emergence of a New Disorder."

2004
The social networking site Facebook is launched and soon becomes one of the most popular social networking sites in the world.

1994
The Caribbean nation of Antigua and Barbuda passes a law allowing online gambling. The first online casinos open; Kimberly Young develops the Internet Addiction Diagnostic Questionnaire, which is used to assess whether people suffer from Internet addiction.

2014
The world-renowned Sundance Film Festival includes two movies about Internet addiction: *Web Junkie*, which examines addiction treatment centers in China, and *Love Child*, about the death of a South Korean couple's baby due to their excessive Internet use.

2010
A South Korean couple's three-month-old daughter dies of malnutrition after they spend hours every day playing online games in an Internet café.

2012
An eighteen-year-old Taiwanese man dies after playing the online game *Diablo III* for forty uninterrupted hours at an Internet café.

2008
China becomes the first country to recognize Internet addiction as a medical condition.

2005

2010

2009
reSTART, the first treatment facility for online addiction in the United States, opens in Fall City, Washington.

2011
The American Society of Addiction Medicine issues a public statement that addiction is a brain disease and can include addiction to behaviors in addition to substances.

2013
The American Psychiatric Association releases an updated version of the *Diagnostic and Statistical Manual of Mental Disorders*, the manual that researchers and clinicians use to diagnose and classify mental disorders; in the back, it includes Internet Use Gaming Disorder as a condition warranting more research. The first hospital-based Internet addiction treatment center in the United States opens at the Bradford Regional Medical Center in Pennsylvania.

Related Organizations

American Gaming Association (AGA)

1299 Pennsylvania Ave. NW, Suite 1175
Washington, DC 20004
phone: (202) 552-2675 • fax: (202) 552-2676
e-mail: info@americangaming.org • website: www.americangaming.org

The AGA's goal is to help create a better understanding of the online gaming entertainment (gambling) industry by providing information to the public, elected officials, other decision makers, and the media. Its website contains articles about online gaming.

American Psychiatric Association (APA)

1000 Wilson Blvd., Suite 1825
Arlington, VA 22209
phone: (703) 907-7300
e-mail: apa@psych.org • website: www.psych.org

The APA is the world's largest professional psychiatric organization and works to provide effective treatment for people with mental disorders. Its website provides information about addiction.

Center for Internet Addiction

PO Box 72
Bradford, PA 16701
phone: (814) 451-2405 • fax: (814) 368-9560
website: www.netaddiction.com

The Center for Internet Addiction counsels individuals, couples, and families concerning problematic Internet use and related issues. Its website offers numerous articles and information sheets about Internet addiction.

Center for Internet and Technology Addiction (CITA)

17 S. Highland St.
West Hartford, CT 06119
phone: (860) 561-8727 • fax: (860) 561-8424
e-mail: drdave@virtual-addiction.com
website: http://virtual-addiction.com

The CITA provides information about addiction to the Internet, social media, and other forms of technology. Its website contains articles, news releases, and lectures by online addiction expert David Greenfield.

GetNetWise

e-mail: cmatsuda@neted.org • website: www.getnetwise.org

GetNetWise is a website created by Internet industry corporations and public interest organizations. It provides information to help ensure that Internet users have safe and constructive online experiences.

Illinois Institute for Addiction Recovery (IIAR)

5409 N. Knoxville Ave.
Peoria, IL 61614
phone: (309) 691-1055
website: www.addictionrecov.org

The IIAR provides treatment for all types of chemical and behavioral addictions, including Internet addiction. Its website offers information about addiction warning signs, effects, and recovery.

Media Smarts

950 Gladstone Ave., Suite 120
Ottawa, ON
Canada K1Y 3E6
phone: (613) 224-7721 • fax: (613) 761-9024
e-mail: info@mediasmarts.ca • website: http://mediasmarts.ca

Media Smarts is a Canadian organization that works to educate young people so that they can develop critical thinking skills and be informed media users. Its website contains news, research, and articles about Internet use.

On-Line Gamers Anonymous

104 Miller Ln.
Harrisburg, PA 17110
phone: (612) 245-1115
e-mail: olga@olganon.org • website: www.olganon.org

On-Line Gamers Anonymous is a fellowship group that works to help people recover from excessive video game playing. Its website offers information about video gaming addiction.

Pew Internet & American Life Project

1615 L St. NW, Suite 700
Washington, DC 20036
phone: (202) 419-4500 • fax: (202) 419-4505
e-mail: info@pewinternet.org • website: http://pewinternet.org

The Pew Internet & American Life Project studies how Americans use the Internet and how it affects them. Its website has the results of numerous studies on social networking and other types of Internet use.

reSTART Internet and Technology Addiction Recovery

1001 290th Ave. SE
Fall City, WA 98024-7403
phone: (800) 682-6934 • fax: (888) 788-3419
e-mail: contactus@netaddictionrecovery.com
website: www.netaddictionrecovery.com

reSTART is a treatment facility whose mission is to help youths and adults recover from Internet and technology addiction. Its website features news articles, personal stories, and other information about addiction to the Internet.

For Further Research

Books

Andrew P. Doan, with Brooke Strickland, *Hooked on Games: The Lure and Cost of Video Game and Internet Addiction*. Coralville, IA: F.E.P. International, 2012.

Samuel C. McQuade et al., *Internet Addiction and Online Gaming*. New York: Chelsea House, 2011.

Alex Soojung-Kim Pang, *The Distraction Addiction: Getting the Information You Need and the Communication You Want Without Enraging Your Family, Annoying Your Colleagues, and Destroying Your Soul*. New York: Little, Brown, 2013.

Hannah O. Price, ed., *Internet Addiction*. Hauppauge, NY: Nova Science, 2011.

Larry D. Rosen, with Nancy A. Cheever and L. Mark Carrier, *iDisorder: Understanding Our Obsession with Technology and Overcoming Its Hold on Us*. New York: Palgrave Macmillan, 2012.

Catherine Steiner-Adair, with Teresa H. Barker, *The Big Disconnect: Protecting Childhood and Family Relationships in the Digital Age*. New York: HarperCollins, 2013.

Kimberly S. Young and Cristiano Nabuco de Abreu, eds., *Internet Addiction: A Handbook and Guide to Evaluation and Treatment*. New Jersey: Wiley, 2011.

Periodicals

Shannon Brys, "Internet Addiction Treatment Programs on the Rise," *Addiction Professional*, September/October 2013.

Hilarie Cash, Cosette D. Rae, Anne H. Steel, and Alexander Winkler, "Internet Addiction: A Brief Summary of Research and Practice," *Current Psychiatry Reviews*, vol. 8, no. 4, 2012.

Bill Davidow, "Exploiting the Neuroscience of Internet Addiction," *Atlantic*, July 2012.

Tony Dokoupil, "Is the Internet Making Us Crazy? What the New Research Says," *Newsweek*, July 9, 2012.

Economist, "Addicted? Really?" March 12, 2011.

Allen Frances, "Internet Addiction: The Next New Fad Diagnosis," *Huffington Post*, August 13, 2012.

Stephen Marche, "Is Facebook Making Us Lonely?" *Atlantic*, May 2012.

Dave Mosher, "High Wired: Does Addictive Internet Use Restructure the Brain?," *Scientific American*. June 17, 2011.

Kevin Roberts, "Confessions of a Cyber-Junkie," *USA Today*, March 2011.

Shosh Shlam and Hilla Medalia, "'China's Web Junkies,'" *New York Times*, January 19, 2014.

Zeynep Tufekci, "Social Media's Small, Positive Role in Human Relationships," *Atlantic*, April 2012.

Sherry Turkle, "The Flight from Conversation," *New York Times*, April 21, 2012.

Alice G. Walton, "Internet Addiction: The New Mental Health Disorder?," *Forbes*, October 2, 2012.

Internet Sources

Bradford Regional Medical Center, Internet Addiction Treatment and Recovery Program, "A Patient and Family Guide," 2013. www.brmc.com/programs-services/BRMC.Family.%20Literature.pdf.

Brandon Griggs, "800 Texts in One Week? Diaries of 3 Smartphone Addicts," CNN, October 9, 2012. http://www.cnn.com/2012/10/05/tech/mobile/smartphone-addicts/.

National Public Radio, "When Playing Video Games Means Sitting on Life's Sidelines," October 20, 2013. www.npr.org/2013/10/20/238095806/when-playing-video-games-means-sitting-on-lifes-sidelines.

Pew Research Center, "Digital Life in 2025: Experts Predict the Internet Will Become 'Like Electricity'—Less Visible, Yet More Deeply Embedded in People's Lives for Good and Ill," March 11, 2014. www

.pewinternet.org/files/2014/03/PIP_Report_Future_of_the_Inter net_Predictions_031114.pdf.

Pew Research Center, "Social Networking Sites and Our Lives," June 16, 2011. www.pewinternet.org/files/old-media/Files/Reports/2011/PIP %20-%20Social%20networking%20sites%20and%20our%20 lives.pdf.

John D. Sutter, "Is 'Gaming Addiction' a Real Disorder?," CNN, August 6, 2012. www.cnn.com/2012/08/05/tech/gaming-gadgets/gaming-add iction-dsm.

Source Notes

Overview

1. Quoted in NewsDesk, "Treating China's Internet Addicts," PBS NewsHour, January 20, 2014. www.pbs.org.
2. Pew Research Center, "Digital Life in 2025: Experts Predict the Internet will Become 'Like Electricity'—Less Visible, Yet More Deeply Embedded in People's Lives for Good and Ill," Pew Research Internet Project, March 11, 2014. www.pewinternet.org.
3. American Psychiatric Association, "Internet Gaming Disorder," *DSM-5 Development*, May 2013. www.dsm5.org.
4. Hilarie Cash, quoted in Elizabeth Cohen, "Does Life Online Give You 'Popcorn Brain'?," CNN, June 23, 2011. www.cnn.com.
5. Allen Frances, "Internet Addiction: The Next New Fad Diagnosis," *Huffington Post*, August 13.2012. www.huffingtonpost.com.
6. Greg Beato, "Internet Addiction," *Reason*, August/September 2010, p. 17.
7. Jacob Forrest, "Why Are MMO's so Addicting?," Giant Bomb, 2010. www.giantbomb.com.
8. David O. Stewart, "Online Gaming Five Years After UIGEA," American Gaming Association, 2011. www.americangaming.org.
9. Bill Davidow, "Exploiting the Neuroscience of Internet Addiction," *Atlantic*, July 2012. www.theatlantic.com.
10. comScore, "It's a Social World: Top 10 Need-to-Knows About Social Networking and Where It's Headed," December 21, 2011. www.comscore.com.
11. Kimberly Young, "Internet Addiction: Questions and Answers," Bradford Regional Medical Center. www.brmc.com.
12. Tony Dokoupil, "Is the Internet Making Us Crazy? What the New Research Says," *Newsweek*, July 9, 2012. www.newsweek.com.
13. Steve Henn, "How Video Games Are Getting Inside Your Head—and Wallet," NPR, October 29, 2013. www.npr.org.
14. Davidow, "Exploiting the Neuroscience of Internet Addiction."

Is Internet and Social Media Addiction a Serious Problem?

15. Hilarie Cash et al., "Internet Addiction: A Brief Summary of Research and Practice," *Current Psychiatry Reviews*, vol. 8, no. 4, 2012, p. 292.
16. Quoted in Ami Schmitz and Jessica Hopper, "Trapped by an Internet 'Addiction,' Obsessed Surfers Seek Rehab Help," *NBC News*, November 8, 2012. http://rockcenter.nbcnews.com.
17. Kimberly Young, "Internet Addiction: Questions and Answers."
18. Andrew P. Doan, with Brooke Strickland, *Hooked on Games: The Lure and Cost of Video Game and Internet Addiction*. Coralville, IA: F.E.P. International, 2012, p. 144.
19. Quoted in Polly Curtis, "Can You Really Be Addicted to the Internet?," *Guardian*, January 12, 2012. www.theguardian.com.
20. Quoted in Schmitz and Hopper, "Trapped by an Internet 'Addiction.'"
21. Quoted in Tamara Lush, "At War with World of Warcraft: An Addict Tells His Story," *Guardian*, August 29, 2011. www.theguardian.com.
22. Quoted in Josh Tapper, "Internet Addicts Face Constant Temptation, Non-Believers,"

Star, February 1, 2013. www.thestar.com.

23. Quoted in Phill Dunn, "Online Gambling Spurs Addiction Fears," *USA Today*, March 16, 2014. www.usatoday.com.

24. Quoted in Stewart, "Online Gaming Five Years After UIGEA."

25. Quoted in Doug Gross, "Have Smartphones Killed Boredom (and Is That Good)?," CNN, September 26, 2012. www.cnn.com.

26. Zeynep Tufekci, "Social Media's Small, Positive Role in Human Relationships," *Atlantic*, April 2012. www.theatlantic.com.

27. Youkyung Lee, "South Korea: 160,000 Kids Between Age 5 and 9 Are Internet-Addicted," *Huffington Post*, November 28, 2012. www.huffingtonpost.com.

What Causes Online Addiction?

28. Recovery.org, "Choosing a Top Internet Addiction Recovery Center." www.recovery.org.

29. Cash et al., "Internet Addiction: A Brief Summary of Research and Practice."

30. Charles O'Brien, interview by John D. Sutter, "Is 'Gaming Addiction' a Real Disorder?," CNN, August 6, 2012. www.cnn.com.

31. Kevin Roberts, "Confessions of a Cyber Junkie," *USA Today*, March 2011. www.usatoday.com.

32. Quoted in AFP RELAXNEWS, "Sundance Film Sheds Light on Chinese 'Web Junkie' Detox Camps," *New York Daily News*, January 24, 2014. www.nydailynews.com.

33. Internet Addiction Resource, "College Students, Young Adults—More Susceptible to Internet Addiction?," April 1, 2014. http://internetaddictionresource.com.

34. Quoted in Shannon Brys, "Internet Addiction Treatment Programs on the Rise," *Addiction Professional*, September/October 2013. www.addictionpro.com.

35. Quoted in Schmitz and Hopper, "Trapped by an Internet 'Addiction,' Obsessed Surfers Seek Rehab Help."

36. Quoted in Carolyn Gregoire, "Welcome to Internet Rehab," *Huffington Post*, September 25, 2013. www.huffingtonpost.com.

37. Quoted in Schmitz and Hopper, "Trapped by an Internet 'Addiction,' Obsessed Surfers Seek Rehab Help."

38. ParentFurther, "Benefits of Online Social Networking." www.parentfurther.com.

39. Sandy Fitzgerald, "Internet Addiction: It's Not Just in Your Head," *2Machines*. www.2machines.com.

How Do Online Addictions Affect Health and Well-Being?

40. Quoted in Schmitz and Hopper, "Trapped by an Internet 'Addiction,' Obsessed Surfers Seek Rehab Help."

41. Tom Stafford, "Does the Internet Rewire your Brain?," BBC, April 24, 2012. www.bbc.com.

42. Roberts, "Confessions of a Cyber Junkie."

43. Jacque Wilson, "Your Smartphone Is a Pain in the Neck," *CNN*, September 20, 2012. www.cnn.com.

44. Quoted in Lindsey Tanner, "Docs Warn About Facebook Use and Teen Depression," *Huffington Post*, March 28, 2011. www.huffingtonpost.com.

45. Jenna Wortham, "Feel Like a Wallflower? Maybe It's Your Facebook Wall," *New York Times*, April 10, 2011. www.nytimes.com.

46. Ira E. Hyman Jr., "Are You Addicted to Your Cell Phone?," *Psychology Today*, March 27, 2013. www.psychologytoday.com.

47. Beth Kassab, "Are You Addicted to Your Smartphone?," *Orlando (FL) Sentinel*, November 25, 2013. http://articles.orlandosentinel.com.

48. Quoted in Sarah Beller, "Internet 'Addiction' Debate Rages On," *The Fix*, November 8, 2012. www.thefix.com.

49. Michael Friedman, "Internet Addiction: A Public Health Crisis?," *Huffington Post*, April 22, 2011. www.huffingtonpost.com.

50. Quoted in Katherine Bindley, "When Children Text All Day, What Happens to Their Social Skills?," *Huffington Post*, December 9, 2011. www.huffingtonpost.com.

51. danah boyd, interview by Emily Bazelon, "Don't Stalk Your Kid Online: An Interview with danah boyd, Author of *It's Complicated: The Social Lives of Networked Teens*," *Slate*, February 2014. www.slate.com.

52. Quoted in Sutter Health, Mills-Peninsula Health Services, "Teens, Computer Addiction and Mental Health." www.mills-peninsula.org.

How Can People Overcome Internet and Social Media Addiction?

53. Campaign for a Commercial-Free Childhood, "What is SFW?," no date. www.screen free.org.

54. Quoted in Caroline Tell, "Step Away from the Phone!," *New York Times*, September 20, 2013. www.nytimes.com.

55. Whitney Mallett, "The Hidden Danger of Internet Addiction Mania: Sketchy Treatment Centers," *Motherboard*, June 7, 2014. http://motherboard.vice.com.

56. Dokoupil, "Is the Internet Making Us Crazy? What the New Research Says."

57. Quoted in Tapper, "Internet Addicts Face Constant Temptation."

58. Quoted in Schmitz and Hopper, "Trapped by an Internet 'Addiction,' Obsessed Surfers Seek Rehab Help."

59. Quoted in PBS, "Treating China's Internet Addicts," January 20, 2014. www.pbs.org.

60. Rebecca J. Rosen, "Can You Get Treatment for Your Internet Addiction?," *Atlantic*, August 2011. www.theatlantic.com.

61. Bradford Regional Medical Center Internet Addiction Treatment and Recovery Program, "A Patient and Family Guide," 2013. www.brmc.com.

62. Quoted in Shosh Shlam and Hilla Medalia, "'China's Web Junkies.'" *New York Times*, January 19, 2014. www.nytimes.com.

63. Quoted in "'China's Web Junkies.'"

64. Todd Essig, "Over-Stimulated: Staying Human in a Post-Human World," *Psychology Today*, February 15, 2010. www.psychologytoday.com.

List of Illustrations

Is Internet and Social Media Addiction a Serious Problem?
Online Technology Affects Relationships   31
Signs of Addiction Are Common   32
Internet Takes Highest Priority in People's Lives   33

What Causes Online Addiction?
Five Traits That Drive Social Media Use   44
Mobile Phones Fuel Addiction   45

How Do Online Addictions Affect Health and Well-Being?
Most People Believe the Internet Is Beneficial   57
Teens Say Social Networking Is a Positive Experience   58
Internet Addicts Exhibit Anxiety and Depression   59
Many People Worry About Reliance on the Internet   60

How Can People Overcome Internet and Social Media Addiction?
Addiction Treatment Shows Success   72
Cognitive Behavior Therapy Has Proved Effective   73
The Challenges of Unplugging   74

Index

Note: Boldface page numbers indicate illustrations.

Abolt, Abby, 49
Aboujaoude, Elias, 23–24, 37–38
addiction
    defining, 11, 18
    dependence factor, 21
    dopamine and, 13
    in *DSM,* 13
    is proven by effects of habit, 24
    profiting from, 9, 18–19
    See also gaming addiction; Internet Addiction Disorder (IAD)
Addiction Research & Theory (journal), 43
Addictive Behaviors (journal), 43
adolescents. *See* youth
age
    is factor
        for Chinese youth, 36, 43
        for middle and high school students, 44
        for those younger than thirty years, 46
    is not factor, 42
    See also youth
Akhter, Noreen, 55
alcohol, social media as more addicting than, 30
American Gaming Association (AGA), 15–16, 24
American Journal of Drug and Alcohol Abuse, 22
American Psychological Association (APA), 13
Anderson, Kent, 10
antidepressants for treating gaming addiction, 75
anxiety
    caused by stopping Internet use, 8
    relationship to IAD, 56, **59**
        causes of, 65
    is result of, 54, 55
    is symptom of, 17
    youth and risk for, 43
Argentina, **74**
Asia, 8, 22
    preventive education in, 63
    smartphone addiction in, 33
    treatment in, 9, 10, 19
Austin, Michael W., 69

Beato, Greg, 15
Becker, Dan, 52
behavioral addiction in *DSM,* 13
Berners-Lee, Tim, 53
boot camps as treatment, 9, 10, 15, 65–66
Boston Consulting Group, 72
boyd, danah, 52
Bradford Regional Medical Center, 18, 21, 66
brain
    changes with large periods of Internet use, 48
    and genetic factors, 17, 35
    and neurotransmitter dopamine, 13–14, 35
    research needed, 35
Business Week (magazine), 60

Carrier, L. Mark, 54
Cash, Hilarie
    on gender and IAD, 36–37
    on inclusion of IAD in *DSM,* 68
    on Internet and the human need to be social, 38
    on learning how to manage Internet use, 63
    on negative effect on face-to-face relationships, 50–51
    on rewards of Internet use, 14
    on variance of worldwide IAD prevalence estimates, 30

cause(s), 9, 17
  different than other media in type of
    engagement, 37–38
  dysfunctional families as, 43, 56
  emotional problems as, 65
  escape from reality as, 35–36, 43
  evidence of, is anecdotal, 35
  gender and, 36–37
  genetic, 35, 37, 41
  lack of willpower as, 40, 65
  large blocks of free time as, 36, 41
  mental health issues as, **44,** 65, 71
  neurochemical reaction as, 35, 40
  pressure on children as, 36, 43
  shyness as, 43
  stress as, 43, 65
Center for Internet Addiction, 12, 36, 75
Cheever, Nancy A., 54
Chen Rong-yu, 23
children. *See* youth
Chile, **74**
China
  gamers in, 15
  prevalence in, 22
  results of refraining from Internet use
    study in, **74**
  treatment in, 10, 19, 65–66, **73**
  youth and risk in, 36, 43
China Daily, 22
Christakis, Dimitri A., 41
Clarke-Pearson, Kathleen, 54
cognitive behavioral therapy (CBT),
  64–65, 70, **73**
cold-turkey treatment, 69
college, free time at, 36, 41
Computers in Human Behavior (journal),
  43, 46, 57, 60
comScore, 16
Current Psychiatry Reviews, 20–21

Davidow, Bill, 16, 19
Daxing Boot Camp (China), 65–66
deaths, 23, 49, 66
Deng Sanshan, 66
depression
  caused by IAD, 49–50, 54

caused by stopping Internet use, 8
  as cause of IAD, 65
  IAD is symptom of, 17
*Diagnostic and Statistical Manual of
  Mental Disorders (DSM),* 13, 68
discipline, lack of, 65
Doan, Andrew P., 21–22, 28
Dokoupil, Tony, 18, 47, 63
dopamine, 13–14, 35
Douthat, Ross, 53

education, 42, 62–63
effects
  negative, of IAD, 9, 10
    academic problems as, 55
    brain changes as, 48
    inability to focus as, 54
    mental health and, 50, 55, 56
    physical, 48–49, 55
  positive, of Internet use, 47, 54, 56
  See also relationships, face-to-face
e-mail, 60
emotional problems. *See* mental health
  issues
escapism, 43
Essig, Todd, 67, 68
ethnicity, 42
Europe, 22, **73, 74**
Everquest (MMORPG), 15
*Experimental and Clinical
  Psychopharmacology* (journal), 75

Facebook
  daily frequency of visits to, 30
  facilitates friendships, 16
  negatively affects academics, 60
  number of members of, 17
Facebook Depression, 54
Fairleigh Dickinson University, 30
families
  and divorce, 46
  dysfunctional, 43, 56
  and parents as punitive and not
    supportive, 57
  single-parent, 46
  and socioeconomic level of parents, 42

Fishman, Dean, 49

Fitzgerald, Sandy, 39

Frances, Allen

on Internet use as enjoyment and not addiction, 14, 21, 28

opposition of, to *DSM* recognition of IAD as medical disorder, 21

on positive aspects of Internet use, 47

Freedom (program), 62

Friedman, Michael, 51, 55

gambling. *See* online gambling

gaming addiction

antidepressant medication as treatment for, 75

and behavior of gamers and cocaine junkies compared, 21

and characteristics of games, 15

examples of, 23, 28, 47–48

friendships made during, 51

gender and, 43

increase in, 28

time spent and likelihood of, 46

gender

and females with underlying emotional problems, 71

is not factor, 37, 41, 42

and males are more likely to be addicted, 36–37, 41, 43, 44

General Hospital Psychiatry (journal), 56

genetics, 17, 35, 37, 41

Goel, Deepak, 41

Goldberg, Ivan, 20

Gorlinski, Lana, 40

Greece, CBT treatment in, **73**

Greenfield, David, 27

Gregoire, Carolyn, 34

Griffiths, Mark D., 22

Guild Wars (MMORPG), 15

Hampton, Keith, 20

Harris Interactive, 39

Havas Worldwide, 71

health insurance, 9, 66

Henn, Steve, 18–19

Heo, Jongho, 42

Hinders, Dana, 42

Hyman, Ira E., Jr., 50

income, 42

Instagram, 16

International Journal of Mental Health and Addiction, 43, 44, 71

Internet Addiction Disorder (IAD)

can affect anyone, 34

creation of, 20

does exist, 14–15

in Asia. *See* Asia

dopamine release and, 14

and is most dangerous addiction, 63

and symptoms are similar to other addictions, 21–22, 28, **32, 33**

does not exist, 8, 14, 40, 65

is not recognized by American medical community, 10, 12–13

and all new technologies have been feared, 38

insurance coverage and, 66

and more evidence is needed, 8, 27, 52

possibility of, 8, 14–15

self-assessment test for, 11–12

should be recognized, 68

should not be recognized, 68

and is symptom of other problems, 17, 67

overuse is not addiction and, 21

smartphones and, 33, 39

sufferers with other addictions, 38, 75

See also gaming addiction

Internet Addiction Resource, 36

Internet use

amount of, 11

and average time spent on, 33

increase in, 33

managing, 63

setting limits to, 62

social media and, 16, 17

by youth, 57

anxiety and depression caused by stopping, 8

emphasis placed on, by society, 75

negative aspects of, 47
as part of US economy, 72
positive aspects of, 47
public opinion about, **57, 60**
reasons for, 71
refraining from, 61–62, **74**
rewards, 13–14
Internet Use Gaming Disorder, 13

Jelenchick, Lauren, 41
Journal of Adolescence, 57

Kaiser Family Foundation, 75
Kamath, Ravinda, 41
Kaneez, Fatima Shad, 70
Kassab, Beth, 50
Kawachi, Ichiro, 42
Kim, Yoon, 42

Lebanon, **74**
Lee, Youkyung, 25
Lehenbauer-Baum, Mario, 29
LinkedIn, 16

Mallett, Whitney, 62–63
Massively Multiplayer Online Role-
    Playing Games (MMORPGs), 15
Medalia, Hilla, 10, 65–66
Melber, Ari, 62
mental health issues
    as cause, **44,** 65, 71
    IAD is symptom of, 17, 38, 43, 65, 67
    IAD often coexists with, 38
    negative effects of, 50, 55, 56
Mexico, **74**
military-style boot camps as treatment,
    9, 10, 65
Mirarchi, Charles "C.P.", 24
mobile phones. *See* smartphones
Montag, Christian, 41
Moreno, Megan M., 41
Myaing, Mon T., 41

New York Times (newspaper), 71

O'Brien, Charles, 27, 35

Oh, Juhwan, 42
O'Keeffe, Gwenn Schurgin, 54
online gambling
    and absence of physical barriers of
        gambling casinos, 16, 24
    addiction, 15–16
    can be regulated, 29
    illegality of, 15–16, 24
    support for legalizing, 30
Orsal, Ozgul, 54
Orsal, Ozlem, 54
Orteg, Melissa, 51–52
Osborne, Lisa A., 41
Osman, Nurul Bahriah Haji, 70
Ozalp, S. Sinan, 54

parents
    divorced, 46
    as punitive and not supportive, 57
    and single-parent families, 46
    socioeconomic status of, 42
Park Jung-in, 25
Petric, Daniel, 22
Pew Research Center
    on effect on face-to-face relationships,
        56
    on frequency of Facebook visits, 30
    on need for Internet access, 71
    on percent of Americans having
        smartphones, 46
    on percent of Americans not online,
        30
    prediction about prevalence of use, 11
    on social media use, 16
PLOS ONE (journal), 56
prevalence
    of addiction, 8, 22
        in Asia, 25–26
        estimates of, 12
        is increasing, 28
        is overstated, 22
        to social media, 16, 17
        worldwide estimates of, vary greatly,
            30
    of Internet use, 8, 10, 30
preventive education, 62–63

Psychiatry Research (journal), 56
Psychological Science (journal), 30

Qihang Salvation Training Camp
    (China), 66
Qualcomm, 39, 46, 75

Rae, Cosette Dawna, 63, 68
Recovery.org, 34
Reed, Alexandra, 25
Reed, Phil, 41
relationships, face-to-face
    constant connection is new form of, 50
    and Internet as only way to socialize,
        52
    negatively affected by Internet, **31**
        and isolation, 53
        and escapism, 36
        real world is ignored and, 50–51
        weaken ties, 56
        and failure of youth to learn needed
            skills, 51–52
    positively affected by Internet, **31**
        allow sociability for fearful, 38
        Internet facilitates, 16, 38–39
        Internet strengthens, 53
        and new friendships, 16, 51
        social media strengthens, 25
        strengthen ties, 56
research
        to determine if IAD exists, 27, 28
        on effects on brain, 35
        on impact of Internet use, 52, 55
        needs, 70
        on treatment, 64
    results on effects of refraining from
        Internet use, **74**
Research and Health (journal), 43
reSTART
    cost of, 66
    effectiveness of, 71, 72, **72**
    male only, 37
    treatment of gamers, 15
Roberts, Kevin, 28, 35–36, 48–49
Romano, Michela, 41
Rosen, Larry D., 20, 54

Rosen, Rebecca J., 64

Schwarz, Tony, 38
Screen-Free Week, 61–62
self-esteem, 18, 56
Shlam, Shosh, 10, 36, 65–66
shyness, 43
Slovakia, **74**
smartphone(s)
    addiction in South Korea, 25–26, 33
    breaks from, 71
    frequency of checking, 39, **45**, 46
    fuel IAD, 39
    percent of adults owning, 46
    physical problems from using, 49
social media use
    addiction
        is similar to hard drugs, 28
        is stronger than to alcohol or
            tobacco, 30
        negative effects of, 49–50, 54
        psychological causes of, **44**
        symptoms, 24–25
    appeal of, 16
    does not cause unhappiness and
        depression, 50
    is positive, 25, **58**
    prevalence of, 16, 17
social networking. *See* social media use
South Korea
    prevalence of IAD in, 25–26, 71
    preventive education in, 63
    smartphone addiction in, 33
    treatment in, 19
Stafford, Tom, 48
Steel, Anne, 68
Stewart, David O., 29
stress
    caused by IAD, 50, 55
    as cause of IAD, 43, 65
Subramanian, S.V., 42
Subramanyam, Alka, 41
symptom(s)
    of IAD, 8, 21
    IAD as, of mental health issues, 17,
        38, 43, 67

Szalavitz, Maia, 69

Taiwan, gaming addiction in, 23
Taylor, Jim, 40, 54
teenagers. *See* youth
Telecommunication Development Sector
  (UN), 30
text neck, 49
Tie, Liming, 70
Time (magazine), 39, 46, 75
tobacco, social media as more addicting
  than, 30
treatment, 9
  antidepressant medication for gaming
    addiction, 75
  cognitive behavioral therapy, 64–65,
    70, **73**
  cold-turkey, 69
  cost of, 66
  effectiveness of, 64, 66, 71, **72, 73**
  gender and, 71
  inpatient, 69
    Bradford Regional Medical Center
      and, 18
    need increase in number of, 64
    See also reSTART
  insurance coverage for, 9, 66
  learning how to manage Internet use is
    essential, 63
  military-style boot camps as, 9, 10, 65
  of underlying issues is essential, 61, 69
Truzoli, Roberto, 41
Tufekci, Zeynep, 25

Uganda, **74**
unhappiness, caused by social media
  addiction, 49–50, 54
United Kingdom, **74**
United States
  Internet as part of economy of, 72
  prevalence of IAD in, 22
  prevalence of Internet use in, 10
  results of refraining from Internet use
    study in, **74**

treatment in, 64
University of Bonn (Germany), 37
Unsal, Alaettin, 54

Van Cleave, Ryan, 23
video game addiction. *See* gaming
  addiction

Walker, Brett, 47–48
Web Junkie (documentary film), 10,
  65–66
willpower, lack of, 65
Wilson, Jacque, 49
Wincent, Patrik, 70
Winkler, Alexander, 68
World of Warcraft (MMORPG), 15, 23,
  43, 47–48
Wortham, Jenna, 49–50

Young, Kimberly S.
  on inpatient treatment, 69
  on recovery, 61
  on self-assessment test for IAD, 11–12
  on treatment in United States, 64
  use of cognitive behavioral therapy by,
    64–65
youth
  amount of Internet use by, 57
  with IAD, 43, 46
    in China, 36, 43
    college, 36
    decrease in prevalence of, in South
      Korea, 71
    educating about dangers of, 62–63
    failure of, to learn social skills,
      51–52
    gender and, 43, 44, 71
    negative academic effects on, 60
  and results of refraining from Internet
    use study, **74**
  time spent consuming media by, 75

Zhou, Chuan, 41
Zhu, Kejing, 70

About the Author

Andrea C. Nakaya, a native of New Zealand, holds a BA in English and an MA in communications from San Diego State University. She has written and edited more than thirty books on current issues. She currently lives in Encinitas, California, with her husband and their two children, Natalie and Shane.